BEADING WITH CHARMS

BEADING WITH CHARMS

Beautiful Jewelry, Simple Techniques

Katherine Duncan Aimone

CONTRA COSTA COUNTY LIBRARY

LARK BOOKS

3 1901 04382 2826

Sterling Publishing Co., Inc.
New York / London

Technical Writer & Editor: **Susan Huxley**

Art Director: **Susan McBride**

Cover Designer: **Cindy LaBreacht**

Associate Art Director: **Shannon Yokeley**

Art Production Assistant: **Jeff Hamilton**

Editorial Assistance: **Mark Bloom**
   and Cassie Moore

Illustrator: **Bonnie Brooks**
   and J'aime Allene

Photographer: **Stewart O'Shields**

Library of Congress Cataloging-in-Publication Data

Duncan-Aimone, Katherine.
  Beading with charms : beautiful jewelry, simple techniques / Katherine
Duncan Aimone. — 1st ed.
    p. cm.
  Includes index.
  ISBN-13: 978-1-60059-019-1 (hc-plc with jacket : alk. paper)
  ISBN-10: 1-60059-019-5 (hc-plc with jacket : alk. paper)
1. Beadwork. 2. Charms (Ornaments) 3. Charm bracelets. I. Title.
  TT860.D844 2007
  745.594'2—dc22
                                              2007013076

10 9 8 7 6 5 4 3 2 1

First Edition

Published by Lark Books, A Division of
Sterling Publishing Co., Inc.
387 Park Avenue South, New York, N.Y. 10016

Text © 2007, Lark Books
Photography © 2007, Lark Books
Illustrations © 2007, Lark Books

Distributed in Canada by Sterling Publishing,
c/o Canadian Manda Group, 165 Dufferin Street
Toronto, Ontario, Canada M6K 3H6

Distributed in the United Kingdom by GMC Distribution Services,
Castle Place, 166 High Street, Lewes, East Sussex, England BN7 1XU

Distributed in Australia by Capricorn Link (Australia) Pty Ltd.,
P.O. Box 704, Windsor, NSW 2756 Australia

If you have questions or comments about this book, please contact:
Lark Books
67 Broadway
Asheville, NC 28801
(828) 253-0467

Manufactured in China

ISBN 13: 978-1-60059-019-1
ISBN 10: 1-60059-019-5

For information about custom editions, special sales, premium and corporate purchases, please
contact Sterling Special Sales Department at 800-805-5489 or specialsales@sterlingpub.com.

CONTENTS

Introduction 6

Getting Started 8
    Before You Begin 8
    Charms 9
    Beads 10
    Wire. 12
    Chain 13
    Findings 14
    Tools and Supplies 15

Techniques 16
    Attaching Charms 16
    Using Jump Rings 16
    Rolling Simple Loops 17
    Making Wrapped Loops 17
    Making Triangular Wraps 18
    Reaming Beads 18
    Drilling Holes in Metal 19
    Using Crimp Beads and Tubes............19
    Tying Knots..20
    Personalizing Fit 20

Beginner Projects 21
    Fairy Garden...22
    Never Too Many 24
    Waterfall..26
    Vintage 28
    Bold and Beautiful 31
    Paris...34
    Southwest..36
    Trinkets..38
    Faces 40

    Rocker Chic 42
    Outrageous 44
    Flower Power...47
    Pennies from Heaven 50

Intermediate Projects................................53
    Mementos 54
    Eclectic..56
    Springtime...58
    Fiesta 61
    Grammy's Baubles 64
    Olde World..67
    Divine 70
    Sunset..72
    Whirlpool 74
    Talisman 78
    Droplets 82
    Waves 84
    Flight of Fancy......................................88
    Heart to Heart 92
    Yee Haw..96
    Forever Yours 100
    True Love 104
    City Nights 108
    Woodland 110
    Northern Lights.....................................113
    Talking Leaves.......................................116
    Orient Express 120

Appendix: Bead, Crystal, and Pearl Shapes 124
Appendix: Standard Stone and Bead Sizes 124
Designers...125
Index..127

Introduction

Welcome to the world of contemporary charm jewelry! The pieces in this book will open your eyes to the many exciting possibilities of using charms to make innovative and interesting adornments. As you thumb through the 35 projects created by 21 top designers, you'll see how easily you can blend traditional ideas about charms with the inventiveness of today's jewelry art.

Perhaps you're interested in assembling a collection of charms that you inherited long ago, or maybe you simply need an "excuse" to spend more time hunting for special charms in bead stores and on the Internet. Maybe you're one to secretly horde small objects—such as subway tokens, coins, or other memorabilia—but you've never discovered a creative way to use them.

The work of jewelry artist Susan Lenart Kazmer provides an example of how to use found objects and materials to make charm-like forms (page 78). Other designers have also followed this popular notion: Terry Taylor uses imprinted souvenir pennies to create a striking wrist piece (page 44), and Andrea Trbovich arranges repurposed vintage earrings and baubles into a glamorous bracelet (page 64).

Each charm creation in this book reflects the individual who designed it. You'll find many examples to whet your own creative urges—including bracelets, bangles, necklaces, earrings, and pins. The variety of charms and materials used in these pieces is truly inspiring. You'll see funky shoe-shaped charms cut from shrink plastic, bright felt flowers, buttons filled with small photos, and tiny toys from a box of candy—all adapted as charms.

Carol McGoogan's Paris-themed bracelet pictured on the cover is a shining example of using charms in new ways. After finding an intriguing chain on a trip, she artfully combined it with themed charms and old chandelier crystals to commemorate her visit to "The City of Light." Erikia Ghumm disassembled a plain heart locket necklace before adding charms and chains to it, creating an entirely new piece (page 104). Both of these examples are rather simple to make, proving that you really don't have to be an experienced beader or jewelry artisan to make intriguing charm jewelry.

To supply you with basic assistance, the front section of the book covers the tools and often-used materials you'll need, as well as techniques for assembling. When you place a group of charms on a piece of jewelry for the first time, you'll begin to understand how personal a designer's choices can be and what an impact a few visual notes can have.

Some designs will require you to follow the instructions accurately, while others encourage you to allow the design to unfold as you work. In either case, you can follow the specific instructions provided for each project or use them as a launching point to make your own variations.

For seasoned beaders and jewelers, there are plenty of challenging and stimulating projects that combine unusual techniques and materials. For example, Tina Koyama uses an undulating herringbone stitch to bead a bracelet with a weave punctuated with protruding beads that serve as charms (page 84). Ndidi Kowalczyk's bold locket collar with trinkets is made with multiple stands of memory wire that allow the piece to evolve as you make it (page 88). And Linda Larsen uses microscope slides and a foiling technique to create focal charms holding delicate flower petals (page 100).

These projects are literally charm-filled, and they will constantly surprise you. This latest entry in Lark's popular *Beading With* series goes way beyond the familiar charm bracelet; it features unique pieces that are fresh, fashionable, fabulous, and fun.

Getting Started

The gorgeous pieces featured in this book probably have you eager to start playing with your tools and bead stash. Whether you use the designs as launching points for your own creations or want to achieve the exact same results, you may find it beneficial to review the information in the following pages.

The content is intended to be a primer, explaining in detail the materials and tools that are used to create the projects. You will find helpful tips and advice to ensure your chances of success, as well as guidance for all of the basic techniques.

One of the joys of making jewelry is choosing your supplies from the tremendous variety of beads, charms, findings, pearls, and types of wire that are on the market. Yet the pleasurable pursuit of supplies can also be a source of frustration, particularly if you are new to this craft. Visiting a bead shop, looking through a catalog, or shopping on a website makes it immediately clear that there are many decisions to make.

The Materials entries for each project in this book ease this process. You'll learn the wire gauge; size and shape of beads, crystals, and pearls; type and size of findings; recommended metal; link size for chains; and many other details that will help you achieve a look similar to the piece that is featured in the accompanying photograph. The Materials entries do, however, make some assumptions, which follow:

- All wire is round, unless specified otherwise.
- Jump ring measurements are the outer diameter.
- Charm measurements are length only.
- Beads, crystals, and pearls are length-drilled unless specified otherwise.
- A charm already has a loop attached at the top; beads, stones, or any other object not called a charm in the materials list will need to be wrapped or threaded in order to attach to a bracelet or neck lace chain, or ear wire.

Keep in mind that you might not be able to find an exact match for a vintage chain, finding, or piece of jewelry. In these situations, trust your sense of design and color, as well as your taste, to find a substitution. The same approach can also be applied to any of the beads.

Charms

Seasoned jewelry makers use the term *charm* rather loosely. They can be referring to a single object or a collection of objects that are treated as a single item. A charm can be beads on a head pin or attached to a small length of chain, a shape cast in metal, or even an interesting item that was never intended to be jewelry, called a *found* object.

Regardless of what a designer considers a charm, all have one thing in common: a charm is attached, usually by only one spot, so it dangles on the finished piece of jewelry.

In this book, however, a charm entry in a materials list refers to an object that already has a loop at the top. This narrow definition is just for clarity—do not let it limit your imagination about what can become a charm on a bracelet, earring, or necklace.

Indeed, just flipping through the pages of this book will confirm that a charm can be almost any little object, and that they are often expressions of personality or interests, or a memento from an important event. Terry Taylor uses pennies that he collects during his travels, as shown on page 50. Several designers like to repurpose vintage jewelry. Andrea Trbovich, for example, hangs over-the-top chunky earrings on old necklace chain. Many designers include dangles made from spectacular gemstones or bead stacks. Other pieces, such as Marlynn McNutt's Southwest (page 36) feature traditional charms.

Susan Lenart Kazmer and Linda Larsen both push the concept of charms to the extreme, using pieces of riveted metal or safety pins for Talisman (far left). Other designers favor game pieces, toys from candy boxes, and clothing buttons. These designers are working with found objects. If this approach appeals to you, make a point to look at the shapes and colors of small items that you encounter as you go through your daily routines; or take a chance in a junk shop and leave with a cigar box loaded with a mishmash of, well, stuff. In short order you will discover that you are drawn to particular items, and that the muse within you has a distinct personality.

Now all you have to do is figure out how to attach these wonderful items to your bracelet or necklace chain, or ear wire. Designers whose pieces are showcased in this book have some ingenious solutions. You can see these by examining the photos, and by reading the step-by-step instructions. The more basic techniques are explained in this section of the book, starting on page 16.

With just a few exceptions, most of the jewelry featured in this book include beads of many types: crystal, glass, metal, pearl, plastic, resin, and semiprecious stone. These beads are treated as charms, focal points, or used to enhance the dominant colors, shapes, textures, and themes of a piece.

The surfaces can be smooth, textured, cut to many angles (*faceted*), or feature a special effect, such as the rich colors in a vitrail crystal. Fire polish beads are a great alternative to higher-priced leaded crystals. They are typically sized from 3 to 12 mm. (There are larger sizes but they are not as readily available.) Fire polish beads are also available in a wide range of colors.

You may already have a wonderful collection of items to play with, or you can purchase supplies that closely resemble the pieces shown in the photographs. There are many Internet sites that sell items that you need or you can surround yourself with beauty by selecting your beads, crystals, and pearls during a visit to a bead shop or show.

Beads can be purchased individually or on a length of cord, or *strand*. Strands are usually 16 inches (40.6 cm) long. Depending on the product, all of the items on the strand can be a single size, or there can be some variation. For this reason, it can be difficult to determine the number of beads on a strand.

Shapes

Unless you sell jewelry supplies—or work in some other part of the industry—you may not be familiar with the many colors, finishes, and shapes that beads come in. There are some common shapes that beginners learn to recognize fairly quickly, such as the bicone (diamond), the teardrop, and the nugget (irregular). To help you sort out the rest, there is a visual guide that begins on page 124. You can also look at the photos of the jewelry pieces for additional guidance.

Sizes

All of the projects in this book include the metric unit measurement of the beads, crystals, and pearls that you need. With the exception of seed beads, which will be discussed in short order, the specified size is the diameter.

More than one designer whose work is featured in this book admitted that a few beads on their pieces were happy accidents. In one case, a bead was just a cast-off that was picked up off the floor. If you already have a treasure trove of beads, crystals, and pearls on hand, you might want to use some of your stash when working on a project that is featured in this book. To make sure that your items are in the same ballpark for size, compare them to the reference guide Standard Stone and Bead Sizes on page 124.

Length drilled

Top drilled

Length drilled

Horizontal drilled

Seed Beads

The workhorse of jewelry making, these tiny beauties are sold in a vast array of colors, finishes, and materials. You can purchase seed beads in small packets at craft stores, but the most common packaging is tubes and strands. If your design calls for stringing a length of seed beads, such as Fiesta on page 61, purchase a strand of seed beads. It is much easier to string the beads onto the beading wire by transferring them directly from the strand. Another alternative is holding a threaded needle in a bead spinner full of loose beads. As you spin the bowl, the beads will slide onto the needle.

Seed bead sizing is slightly different than other beads. The lower the number, the larger the bead. For example, an 8° is chunky in comparison to an 11°.

Like other beads, seed beads come in a variety of shapes, from oval (rocaille), to square, hexagonal, and triangular. Size, shape, and the hole can be unpredictable, although some manufacturers—or even the country of origin—are noted for the uniformity of their products.

Delica beads fall into this category. Produced by the Miyuki company in Japan, there are now other companies creating similar products. Delica beads are well-known for their consistent sizing, larger holes, and straight sides that are ideal for stringing rows.

Drill

Some beads need to be tested for fit on the wire or findings of choice. The position and size of the hole, or *drill*, in the bead, crystal, or pearl will have a huge effect on the finished piece because it determines how the object will be attached.

A bead with a hole that runs from the top to the bottom is called length-drilled. This is the most common treatment. You can assume that supplies lists are calling for a length-drilled bead, crystal, or stone if nothing is specified.

When the hole is through the width, it is a horizontal drill.

As the name implies, a top-drilled (or *tip-drilled*) bead, crystal, or pearl has a hole near the top.

The size of a hole is another concern. The beads might need larger holes, in order to use stronger wire or to feed the beads onto a thick item, such as the bangle for Never Too Many (right). Some suppliers might let you request a strand that includes beads with larger holes. Depending on the product, the hole size may not be consistent from one bead to the next. If necessary, you can drill, or *ream*, a hole to make it larger (see Reaming Beads on page 18).

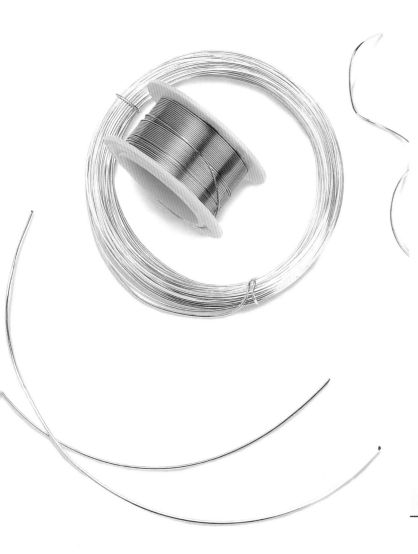

Wire is available as half-hard, soft, and dead-soft. Jewelers gravitate to half-hard and dead-soft. Half-hard wire is stiffer, so it holds its shape better. This is a good choice for wrapped loops. Dead-soft is very easy to shape, so it is a good choice when you want to weave with wire.

As you manipulate wire by bending, wrapping, and hardening it with hammering, it will become firmer. Designer Marie Lee Carter, who created Olde World (page 67) uses dead-soft for everything, and hardens it as she develops the piece.

The type of metal used for the wire determines its color. Some designers prefer all of the metals in a piece to be the same color. Others like the contrast that can be achieved by mixing metals, using sterling silver for head pins and some links, and gold-color or rusted steel wire for inserting wire through a bead (or beads) and making loops at both ends, called a *link*.

Wire is sold in many shapes, including half-round, square, triangular, and twisted. In this book, you can assume that the wire is round, unless the materials entry indicates otherwise.

Designer's Tip

After you snip off a piece of wire or the top of a head pin, take the time to smooth the edge with sandpaper. This will protect delicate skin from damage when you are wearing the piece.

Memory Wire

As the name suggests, this wire has a memory of sorts. It is designed to hold its circular shape. If you try to straighten an end, it will snap back to its original shape as soon as you release it. Obviously, it is strong. For this reason, you need to put some effort into bending a loop at the end, for attaching a clasp. This wire will even nick wire cutters, so you will need special, heavy-duty shears to snip it.

Wire

Size (or *gauge*), hardness, color (or metal), and shape are the wire characteristics you will choose when gathering supplies to make a piece.

In this book, the materials list for each project includes a recommended wire gauge. Dainty beads and charms are usually matched with finer wire. Jewelers will deviate from this rule of thumb when wearability comes into play.

Bracelets, for example, are exposed to considerable wear and tear, so the wires in these pieces need to be thick enough to withstand constant movement.

In this book, the projects call for 14- to 28-gauge wire. The number designations are counterintuitive: the thicker the wire, the lower the gauge.

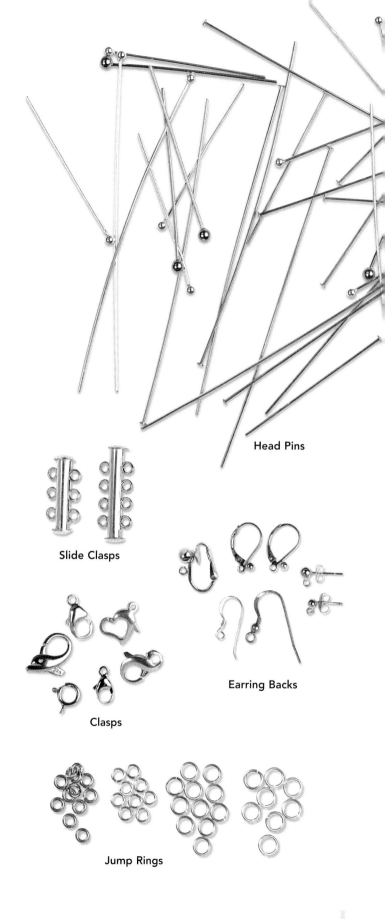

Head Pins

Slide Clasps

Earring Backs

Clasps

Jump Rings

Chain

You can purchase chain in bead shops or on Internet websites. It is usually sold in spools. Jewelers often have a collection of chain types and sizes in their stash. As they design a piece, they'll pick from their collection, snipping off the lengths they want. You can see the result of this creative blending in many of the pieces in this book. The effect, as you can see in Woodland (page 110), is striking.

If you want a clasp to lay flat, consider your choice of chain carefully, because you can use the last link to connect the clasp, rather than adding a jump ring.

To achieve a look that is similar to the featured pieces in this book, the materials lists include the link size.

Like the flat-head version, a ball-end version has a little tidbit at the end that holds the bead or beads on the head pin. In this case, it is a small bead of metal. You can purchase these as finished findings, or easily make your own with sterling silver, as explained on page 109.

Eye pins can also be purchased ready-made or shaped with wire. The bottom of this type of head pin has a small round loop. This loop can be employed as a decorative effect at the bottom of a dangle, or you can use it as a shortcut when creating a *link*. Simply thread the desired bead or beads (a *bead stack*) onto the eye pin, and roll a loop at the top. Now you have a loop at both the top and the bottom of the eye pin. You can open these up and thread on other dangles, to build a longer piece.

Findings

Prefabricated jewelry parts, such as clasps, ear wires, head pins, jump rings, and split rings, fall into this category.

Clasps

The way that your bracelet or necklace is closed can be an integral part of the design, or simply a functional device. On page 74, Tamara Honoman explains how to make a graceful swan clasp that echoes the swirls and spirals of her piece. In sharp contrast, you might not be able to find the clasp that Jean Campbell attached to her Faces bracelet (page 40) because she believes that clasps should be seen and not heard.

For the most part, the clasp choice is left to you for the projects in the book.

Head Pins

These short lengths of metal are wonderful for hanging beads and charms from chain. There are three types: ball-end, flat-end, and eye pins.

Flat-end is the most common type of head pin. When a type is not specified, you can assume that the head pin is a flat-end. This type has a tiny horizontal bar at the bottom, which spans the hole in a bead to prevent it from falling off. When a bead hole is too large, first slip a seed bead, bead cap, or spacer on the head pin.

Jump Rings

Jump rings are available in many sizes and types of metal, so tracking down what you need is easy. Round jump rings are the norm, but you can find other shapes. Bonnie Clewans calls for an oval jump ring for her Woodland earrings on page 110. In this case—and a few others in the book—these hard-working findings are an integral part of the design.

Large and small jump rings are used to attach bead dangles to the Whirlpool bracelet (page 74). The large jump rings are intentionally positioned at equal intervals along the chain, to add another visual element to the piece.

Jump ring size can be specified by the outer or the inner diameter. This is an important consideration because jump rings are available in more than a few gauges. The difference between the inner and outer diameter will be greater for thicker jump rings.

Designer Marlyn McNutt advocates using thick jump rings any time you are making a bracelet. Thinner jump rings are not as dependable, because they will come open much easier when the finished piece is worn.

To use a jump ring, you must pry it apart where the circle is cut. It is most important that you pull the ends apart in a manner that does not distort the shape. This technique is explained on page 16.

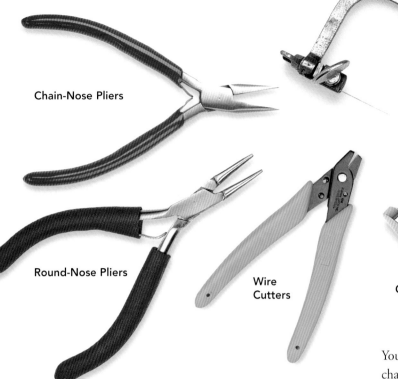

Chain-Nose Pliers

Jeweler's Saw

Round-Nose Pliers

Wire Cutters

Chasing Hammer

Tools and Supplies

Having the right tools for the job can mean the difference between a pleasurable jewelry making experience and a session that ends in frustration. If you're new to this art, you can get by with a few basic tools. As your repertoire of techniques increases, you will find yourself amassing additional tools.

Stocking Up

Here is a list of items that you will find indispensable:

Ball peen hammer
Center punch
Chasing hammer
Fine-tip permanent marker
Flex shaft or handheld rotary tool
Glue with precision applicator
Jeweler's saw
Leather mallet
Ruler with metric equivalents
Safety glasses to use when drilling or handling
   caustic chemicals
Scissors

You might as well pull out your chain-nose pliers, round-nose pliers, and wire cutters every time you sit down at your worktable. These three tools are used in almost all jewelry projects.

If you are purchasing tools for the first time, look for thinner, smaller tools. The best sources are jewelry supply shops and Internet websites, rather than the local hardware store.

Chain-nose pliers are used to open jump rings, bend wire, and act as grabbers when you cannot access an area with your fingers.

The barrel of round-nose pliers tapers toward the tips, so they are ideal for shaping loops of various sizes.

Wire cutters will help you snip through wire and soldered chain links. Start your tool collection with a tiny pair. There are many types of wire cutters, but jewelers tend to prefer flush cutters, which pinch the ends as they cut.

Try to purchase cutters that are treated for the maximum gauge of wire that you plan to work with. Later, pick up some heavy-duty wire cutters for more demanding jobs, or when precision is not an issue.

For one of the toughest jobs, cutting memory wire, you will need cutters that are designed specifically for this purpose. Using your regular wire cutters to snip through memory wire is a good way to ruin them.

Techniques

Throughout this book, you will find instructions calling for you to perform certain techniques, such as rolling a loop. This section of the book will introduce you to these common techniques, or give you the opportunity to brush up on your skills, by following the illustrations and instructions.

Attaching Charms

Position loops and jump rings so that dangles (bead stacks on head pin, or charms) will face front when attached to the chain.

On a link chain bracelet, this means that the dangles should be attached to the lower portion of a link, or to the front of link (figure 1).

fig. 1

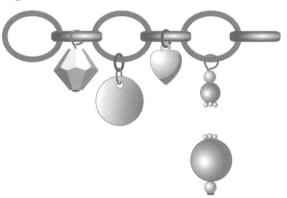

As you connect your charms, the chain can twist. To ensure that the charms face the same direction, reposition the bracelet after you connect each charm.

Designer's Tip

You can change the size of the loop by positioning the wire deeper inside the pliers, where the barrels are wider.

Using Jump Rings

You will find that all jump rings have been cut through somewhere on the perimeter. You use this opening to thread on beads, head pin loops, and other jewelry items. There is a specific technique for opening and closing a jump ring so that the shape is not distorted.

Using two pairs of pliers, grasp each end of the jump ring at the cut (photo 1). Open the jump ring by pulling one side toward you and the other side away from you. If your supplies are limited, use chain-nose pliers and round-nose pliers for this process. The ideal is to use two sets of chain-nose pliers, because round-nose pliers tend to slip. Never pull the ends apart. To close a jump ring, simply reverse the process by twisting the ends back together.

photo 1

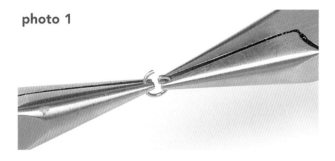

Rolling Simple Loops

A simple loop can be made at the top of a head pin, or at the end of a piece of wire. As you make your first loop, keep in mind that you want it to be round and centered above the beads or charm that are underneath.

1. Thread the desired beads. Above the uppermost item, bend the wire to a 90° angle. Cut off the wire to ⅜-inch (.95 cm) long. Some designers recommend a ¼-inch (.6 cm) length.

2. Grasp the end of the wire in your round-nose pliers (photo 2). Roll the wire around the closed barrels of the pliers until the end of the wire touches the bend (photo 3). Remove the pliers.

photo 2   **photo 3**

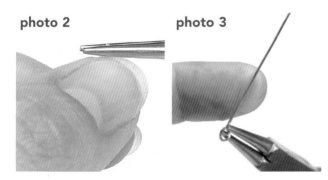

Making Wrapped Loops

Wrapped loops are more durable than simple loops because they are permanent. You do not have to worry about them opening accidentally. The drawback to wrapped loops is that you need to plan the position of your dangles carefully if you want to attach the dangles by the loop in the head pin. (The solution to this disadvantage is to attach dangles by inserting a jump ring through the finished wrapped loop. The jump ring can then be closed around the chain link.)

Here is the process for making a wrapped loop.

1. Use your chain-nose pliers to grasp the wire directly above the last item that you threaded onto it. Bend the wire to a 90° angle (figure 2). Set aside the chain-nose pliers.

2. Grasp the bend in the wire with your round-nose pliers. Wrap the wire around the barrel of the pliers to form half a loop. Reposition the pliers and then complete the rest of the loop (figure 3). Remove the round-nose pliers.

fig. 2   **fig. 3**

   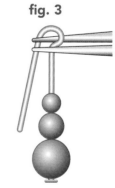

3. With the chain-nose pliers, open the loop just enough to slip it onto the chain link. Close the loop.

4. Wrap the end of the wire around the stem until the wraps reach the top of the bead stack (figures 4 and 5). Cut off the excess wire.

fig. 4   **fig. 5**

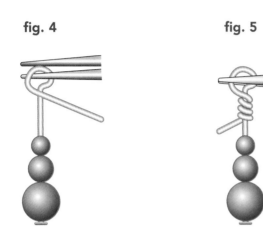

Designer's Tip

You can finish off the tip of the cut wire so the finished piece does not scratch your skin by tucking the end underneath the last wrap. Some designers also squeeze the wrap, which secures the end and also tightens the wraps.

Making Triangular Wraps

Experienced jewelers will recognize this as the wrap they make for a briolette (a tip-drilled oval, pear, or teardrop bead). This same wrap also looks great on a bead that is drilled through the width, or a bicone you want to position horizontally.

1. Cut a piece of wire 2-inches (5 cm) long. With the flat-nose pliers, bend up the last ½ inch (1.3 cm) of the wire. Thread a bead onto the wire.

2. Fold up the other side of the wire until the pieces cross directly above the bead, creating a hat (figure 6).

3. Take the chain-nose pliers to the base of the longer wire, and bend it back down a bit. Use the round-nose pliers to make a simple loop (figure 7).

fig. 6   **fig. 7**

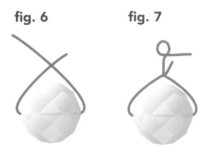

4. Finish the piece by wrapping the end of the longer wire around the base several times. Snip off the excess wire and file the end, or else tuck it underneath the last loop.

Reaming Beads

When the hole in a bead is too small to fit onto a wire, head pin, or finding you can make it larger. It is not worth the effort to ream a seed bead, or any other inexpensive bead. Semiprecious stones or artisan beads, on the other hand, are ideal candidates for this process.

You can use a manual or electric bead reamer.

1. Stick the bead to a small piece of poster putty.

2. Begin reaming. Tips are diamond-coated, so using the reamer dry too often will wear off this surface. Instead, try to keep the tip wet. If using a manual tool, you can work with the reamer submerged in a shallow bowl of water or held under running water. Never do this with an electric reamer. Instead, dip the drill bit in a small cup of water whenever it feels like the bead is sticking. Stop when you are midway through the bead's hole. Work slowly for maximum control, and do not push too hard.

3. Remove the putty, flip the bead over and stick the putty on the opposite side. Finish reaming the hole from the newly exposed opening.

Do not ream crystals. They shatter easily. Instead, choose a jump ring or wire to fit the hole. The jump ring size that fits in the crystal's hole will be sufficient to support the crystal, and will be strong enough to last with regular, everyday wear.

Drilling Holes in Metal

Whether you are making a hole to string an item or make a rivet, the process is basically the same. You can use a flex shaft or an electric, handheld rotary tool. While drilling a hole may take a few moments longer using a manual drill, you have more control.

1. Mark the hole position with a fine-tip permanent pen. (Some jewelers skip this step.) Do not mark the hole position too close to an edge, particularly when working with soft metal such as sterling silver, which can tear when drilled.

2. Place the charm or piece of metal on an anvil. Create a divot at the marked spot. You can do this by positioning the tip of an awl or a center punch at the hole mark, and then tapping the top with a hammer (figure 8).

fig. 8

3. You may want to clamp the item to a piece of wood, to prevent the metal piece from spinning while drilling. Position the tip of the drill bit in the divot and begin drilling. Do not force the drill bit through the metal. Drill slow and steady, letting the drill do the work.

For a thicker item, you might want to start with a drill bit that makes a hole smaller than you need. After creating the first hole, you can enlarge it with a drill bit that is for a hole the desired finished size.

4. After drilling, smooth the rough edges with a file, and then sandpaper.

Using Crimp Beads and Tubes

Crimping creates a loop with beading wire, for attaching a clasp. But you can adapt crimps for other uses, as Bonnie Clewans has done in Fiesta (page 61).

The process starts with either a crimp tube or bead. As you do more crimping, you will find that you prefer one shape over another.

1. Slide the crimp bead or tube onto the beading wire.

2. Turn the wire and insert it back through the crimp bead or tube, starting at the same end from which it just emerged. Leave a small loop of beading wire.

3. Place the crimp bead or tube in the crimp tool and close it (figure 9). When the crimp bead or tool curls slightly, remove it from the crimp tool.

fig. 9

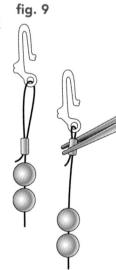

4. Cut the end of the wire at the bottom of the crimp bead or tube. If desired, you can cut it long enough to thread through the closest few beads on the strand.

5. If desired, place the crimp cover around the crimp bead or tube. Grasp the cover with the end of the crimp tool and gently squeeze to secure it.

Tying Knots

You only need to know a few knots to create the pieces that are featured in this book.

Half Hitch Knot

Also known as a simple knot, you make this on a strand of beading cord or thread, next to a bead.

1. Form a loop in the cord, and pass the cord end through the loop (figure 10).

2. Insert the tweezers through the loop and grasp the working cord next to the last bead. Pull the cord gently to slide the loop along the cord until it is next to the bead (figure 11). Pull the knot tightly.

fig. 10   **fig. 11**

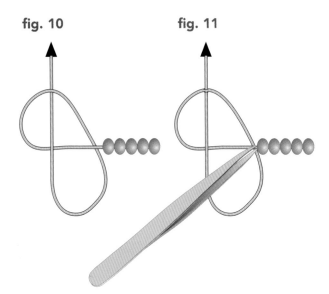

Designer's Tip

The standard length for necklaces are as follows:
Choker: 15 to 16 inches (38. 1 to 40.6 cm)
Princess: 18 inches (45.7 cm)
Matinee: 20 to 26 inches (50.8 to 66 cm)
Opera: 28 to 36 inches (71.1 to 91.4 cm)
Lariate or rope: 48 inches (121.9 cm)

Overhand Knot

You might know this as a granny knot.

1. Form a loop in the cord or thread.

2. Pull the end of the cord that is underneath, through the loop and pull both ends to tighten the knot (figure 12).

fig. 12

Double Knot

This is very similar to an overhand knot.

1. Form a loop in the cord or thread.

2. Bring one end of the cord or thread through the loop, to go over and under the loop. At this point, you have an overhand knot.

3. Do not tighten the knot. Instead, continue by wrapping the same end of the cord or thread over and under the loop a second time.

Personalizing Fit

Do you have slim—or strong—wrists? You might want to tweak the length of your bracelets so that they look just right on your body.

1. Measure your wrist, and allow a bit of slack for a comfortable fit.

2. Subtract the length of the clasp. This gives you the length of chain that you need.

FAIRY GARDEN

A thing of beauty can also be simple. Cavorting fairies and a rainbow of precious crystals are attached to a bracelet using jump rings and simple loops.

Designer: Marlynn McNutt

Finished size: 7½ inches (19 cm)

Materials

6 bicone crystals in capri blue, green, light purple, light yellow, pale brown, and red, 8 mm

5 polygon crystals (top-drilled) in brown, burgundy, light purple, pale blue, and purple, 13 mm

2 AB polygon crystals (top-drilled), 13 mm

2 sterling silver dragonfly charms, 20 mm

Sterling silver dragonfly charm, 14 mm

3 sterling silver fairy charms, 17, 18, and 20 mm

Sterling silver moon goddess, 16 mm

6 sterling silver head pins, 1½ inches (3.8 cm) long

14 sterling silver jump rings, 6.5 mm

7½-inch (19 cm) sterling silver 7 mm bracelet with clasp

Tools

Chain-nose pliers

Needle threader

Ruler

Scissors

Glue

Techniques

Using jump rings (page 16)

Rolling simple loops (page 17)

Instructions

1. Insert a head pin into each of the bicones, and make a simple loop at the top of every one.

2. Twist open all of the jump rings.

3. Slip a large dragonfly charm onto a jump ring and then insert the jump ring through the first link of the bracelet, at the clasp end. Close the jump ring. Attach an AB polygon to the next link of the bracelet in the same manner.

4. Threading jump rings to the charms and polygons and opening the simple loop at the top of each bicone, continue adding crystals and charms to the bracelet. Skip links for attractive spacing, and place the dangles in the following order: the capri blue bicone, largest fairy, purple polygon, light purple bicone, small dragonfly, pale blue polygon, light yellow bicone, moon goddess, brown polygon, green bicone, 17 mm fairy, light purple polygon, red bicone, remaining fairy, burgundy polygon, pale brown bicone, large dragonfly, and AB polygon (figure 1).

fig. 1

NEVER
TOO MANY

Look out scrapbookers! Jewelry makers may raid your supplies for stamps, metallic ink, and shrink film plastic in order to create this fast and fun bangle.

Instructions

1. Stamp six shoes onto the shrink film plastic sheet. Leave a ¾-inch (1.9 cm) border around each stamp. Let the plastic air-dry.

2. Using the paper punch, make holes at the top of each shoe shape. Cut out all of the shoe shapes, leaving a ¼-inch (6 mm) wide border of black plastic around each one (figure 1). Bake the shoes in the oven or toaster oven according to the manufacturer's instructions, in a well-ventilated room.

fig. 1

3. When the charms are cool, glue a crystal to each one.

4. Using the pliers, attach (and close) a jump ring through the hole in each charm. Unscrew a ball from one end of the bracelet. String the charms and furnace glass beads onto the bracelet. Screw the ball back onto the bracelet.

Designer's Tips

Make sure that the jump rings are large enough to slide on the silver bangle but small enough that they do not slip over the ball at each end of the bangle.

If ordering the furnace beads by phone or over the Internet, make sure you ask for beads with large holes. Suppliers will honor this request. If, however, you end up with some pieces that will not fit onto the bracelet, try reaming the beads to make the holes bigger (page 18).

All stamp pads are not created equal. You may have to test out a few brands to find the best one for this bracelet.

If you want to make a lot of these charms, it is best to purchase a toaster oven and not prepare food in it.

Designer: Kristal Wick

Finished size: To fit your purchased
    cuff-style bracelet

Materials

18 large furnace glass beads (large holes)

6 flat-back crystals, 9 mm

6 sterling silver jump rings, 6 mm

Sterling silver cuff-style bracelet (round)
    with removable ball ends, 70 x 50 mm

Pre-inked stamp pad in a permanent
    metallic color

Sheet of black shrink film plastic

Strong jewelry glue

Tools

Chain-nose pliers, 2 pair

Flat metal baking sheet that fits in your
    oven or toaster oven

Oven or toaster oven

Scissors

Shoe motif rubber stamps

Single-hole punch for paper

Techniques

Using Jump Rings (page 16)

Sparkling gems in varying shapes
tumble from simple ear wires.

Instructions

Make two.

1. Cut the silver chain into five sections, varying the lengths from ¾ to 1½ inches (1.9 to 3.8 cm).

2. Place a faceted stone, face down, on a flat surface. Place the setting, also face down, on top of the stone. Press down on the setting until you feel the stone click into it. Check to ensure that the stone is seated properly and adjust it, if necessary. If the stone isn't seated properly the first time, you can try to adjust using a toothpick or remove it and try again. If the prongs don't seem to want to let the stone in, you could use the chain-nose pliers to adjust one prong open to allow the stone to be gripped in place. However, the settings are calibrated and typically are ready for setting!

3. Using the chain-nose pliers, gently squeeze the prongs on both sides of the stone, to only slightly move them (figure 1), working your way around the setting until the stone is secure and all of the prongs are against the stone.

fig. 1

fig. 2

4. Cut a 3-inch (7.6 cm) length of wire. Place your round-nose pliers in the center of the cut length of wire. Begin a wrapped loop but, before wrapping, slip the top of the setting onto the wire. Continue with the wrapped loop, capturing the setting inside it (figure 2). Make another wrapped loop with the remaining section of wire, capturing the last link of one length of chain. Seat the remaining stones in their settings and secure a wrapped loop wire to each one, while attaching a length of chain.

5. Slip the ends of the chains for three stones onto a small jump ring, and close it. Slip two lengths of chain—without stones attached—onto another small jump ring, and close it. Attach a large jump ring to the charm, and close it. Slip the jump rings for the charm and the chain onto another large jump ring, and close it. Slip the lower loop of one ear wire and the jump rings for the dangles onto another large jump ring, and close it.

Materials

Designer: Tamara Honaman

Finished size: 4 inches (10.2 cm)

Citrine oval, 8 mm

Trillion amethyst triangular, 8 mm

Pear peacock topaz, 8 mm

2 coin charms, 20 mm

Oval stone setting, 8 mm

Pear stone setting, 8 mm

Triangular stone setting, 8 mm

6 sterling silver jump rings, 5 mm

4 sterling silver jump rings, 4 mm

2 sterling silver French ear wires with bead

18-inch (45.7 cm) length of 24-gauge sterling silver wire

10-inch (25.4 cm) length of 1.5 mm fine sterling silver rolo chain

Tools

Chain-nose pliers, 2 pair

Round-nose pliers

Wire cutters

Techniques

Making Wrapped Loops (page 17)

Designer's Tips

You know a stone is seated properly in a setting when you can look across the surface of the stone and it reflects the light on an even plane and, if you run your finger across the surface, the stone does not budge.

The set stones are attached to the chain with a double-wrapped loop. This requires more wire than a basic wire-wrap because one loop captures the setting and another connects to a link in the chain.

VINTAGE

Challenge traditional ideas about charms with a necklace made from safety pins, vintage chain, and found objects.

Instructions

Designer: Linda Larsen

Finished size: 24 inches (61 cm)

Materials

9 gray freshwater pearls, 10 mm

13 brass charms, 20 to 30 mm

Vintage metal objects: such as game pieces, keys, locks, bus token, button, and bolt; 12 to 25 mm

36 inches (91.4 cm) brass 18-gauge wire

13 brass safety pins, 1 inch (2.5 cm) long

2 brass safety pins, 1½ inches (3.8 cm) long

Brass safety pin for most of the found objects

Brass jump rings, as needed for found objects

63-inch (157.5 cm) length of vintage 10 mm brass chain

Antiquing, liver of sulphur, or patina solution

Tools

Chain-nose pliers, 2 pair

Round-nose pliers

Wire cutters

Fine-tip permanent marker

Center punch and hammer

Safety glasses

Drill and ¹⁄₁₆-inch (1.6 mm) drill bit

Techniques

Using Jump Rings (page 16)

Reaming Beads (page 18)

Drilling Holes in Metal (page 19)

Note: You may not be able to find some of the exact charms shown in the featured piece. These are found objects that have caught the designer's eye. Use the descriptions—and look at the photos—for inspiration so that you can track down your own special finds.

Instructions

1. Cut three strands of chain to 19, 21, and 23 inches (48.3, 53.3, 58.4 cm) long.

2. Oxidize or apply the antiquing or patina solution to all of the metal: chain, charms, safety pins, and found objects.

3. Feed the last link of the shortest length of chain onto an open, small safety pin. Attach another small safety pin onto the last link of the longest chain. Join the safety pins to make one long length.

4. Grasp a link 1½ inches (3.8 cm) from one end. Slide this link onto one of the large safety pins. Beyond the small safety pins 1 inch (2.5 cm), slide another link onto the remaining large safety pin. Use a small safety pin to attach the loose end of the chain to the first large safety pin (figure 1).

fig. 1

Designer's Tip

You can use a butane or propane torch to darken metal. Place the piece on a fire brick and slowly pass the flame back and forth until you like the color change. You can also bake metal in a toaster oven. After applying a solution to age a metal piece, you can spray a matte sealer to stabilize the finish. This also prevents a finish from rubbing off on clothing.

5. Grasp a link 2 inches (5 cm) from the end of the remaining, 21-inch (53.3 cm) length of chain. Slide this onto the first large safety pin. Slide the last link of the opposite end of this chain onto a small safety pin. Feed this small safety pin through the other large safety pin and close them. Join the two large safety pins, end to end. This will be the clasp.

6. Thread each pearl onto a small safety pin. Use the safety pins to attach the pearls along the chains. Pearls may have to be reamed to fit on the safety pins. If necessary, bend the pins to close around the pearls.

7. Add the charms and found objects randomly along the chains, using safety pins to attach them. If you have something that will not lay right with the safety pin connection, use a jump ring instead. Some pieces may look better if attached with an organic wire wrap that is created by making a loop in the wire with your round-nose pliers, attaching the item, and then bringing up the end of the wire to make a loose wire wrap (figure 2).

fig. 2

8. Make a small divot using the center punch and hammer where you want to place a hole in the token and other metal objects that need a hole. With the back of the token facing you and wearing safety glasses, drill the hole.

BOLD AND BEAUTIFUL

Smooth, platinum-colored freshwater pearls provide a pleasing contrast to rugged, hand-crafted silver crosses.

Designer: Louise McClure

Finished size: 15½ inches (39.4 cm)

Materials

38 freshwater pearls (potato), 8 mm

6 antiqued metal 8° seed beads

3 antiqued metal 6° seed beads

Apatite faceted bead (button, center-drilled), 4 mm

Silver cross charm, 34 mm

Silver cross charm, 55 mm

Silver cross charm, 43 mm

Sterling silver toggle clasp

2 sterling silver crimp tubes, 2 mm

2 sterling silver crimp covers, 3 mm

2½-inch (6.4 cm) length of 26-gauge sterling silver wire, dead soft

45-inch (114.3 cm) length of 3-ply nylon cord

Craft glue with precision applicator

Stick of incense and lighter

(Continued on next page)

Instructions

1. Spread a drop of craft glue on both ends of the cord. You can use the dry, stiff cord ends to pick up the seed beads. Make an overhand knot at the center of the cord. Place an alligator clip to the right of the knot, to prevent the beads from sliding.

2. Pick up 8°, 6°, and 8° seed beads with the left end of the cord and slide the beads to the center knot. Form a half hitch knot next to the last bead on the cord.

3. Still using the left side of the cord, slide the largest cross onto the cord and toward the center. The loop for this charm will sit on top of the seed beads (figure 1).

fig. 1

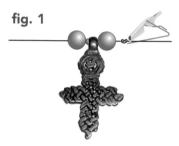

4. Pick up a pearl, slide it toward the center of the cord until it is snug against the seed beads, and form a half hitch knot next to the pearl. Pick up 8°, 6°, and 8° seed beads on the cord, and slide them toward the center until they are snug against the pearl. Form a half hitch knot in the cord, next to the last bead on the cord.

5. Pick up a pearl, slide it toward the center, and form a half hitch knot next to the pearl. Continue adding pearls to the cord, forming a half hitch knot next to each one, until you have 19 pearls on the cord. Place the remaining alligator clip at the end of the cord, snug against the last pearl.

6. Turn the piece. Remove the alligator clip near the center of the cord. Using the right side of the cord, repeat step 4.

7. Thread a cross onto the cord, and slide it toward the center until it is on top of the seed beads. Thread the remaining pearls onto the cord, forming a half hitch knot after each one is in position. Attach an alligator clip to the cord next to the last pearl.

8. Bend one end of the sterling silver wire to form a wrapped loop, adding the remaining cross before closing it. Slide the faceted apatite bead onto the wire, and form a wrapped loop to attach the cross. Position this dangle over the three seed beads to the left of the central cross.

9. Slide a crimp tube onto the end of the cord. Thread the cord through one part of the toggle clasp. Thread the cord end back through the crimp tube, to form a loop. Pin through the loop and into the workboard—adjacent to the toggle clasp—and gently pull the cord end tight. The pin will allow a slight ease in the finished loop. Form a half hitch knot in the cord, next to the crimp tube, and then close the crimp with the crimp pliers. Place a dab of glue on the knot, and let it dry.

10. Cut off the cord end ³⁄₁₆ inch (5 mm) from the knot. Touch the cord end with a lit stick of incense to melt it and prevent fraying. Position a crimp cover over the crimp tube. Tuck in the end of the cord. Close the crimp cover with the tip of the crimp pliers.

11. Remove the alligator clip at the opposite end of the necklace, and attach the remaining part of the closure in the same manner.

PARIS

A chain brought back from the City of Light was the inspiration for this bracelet. To enhance the memory, charms nestle among crystals salvaged from an old chandelier.

Finished size: 7½ inches (19 cm)

Materials

6 chandelier crystals (top- and bottom-drilled),17 mm

6 silver-filled star charms, 5 mm

3 photo frame charms, 18 mm

22 Paris-theme charms: gold, brass, nickel, copper, and silver-filled, 6 to 13 mm

24 brass jump rings, 4 mm

12 brass head pins (optional, see step 1), 2 inches (5 cm) long

Toggle clasp

7-inch (17.8 cm) length of 4 to 6 mm antiqued brass chain

3 photos or pictures, to fit the frame charms

Clear craft lacquer

Clear drying all-purpose glue stick

Tools

Chain-nose pliers, 2 pair

Flat-nose pliers

Round-nose pliers

Wire cutters

Scissors

Paintbrush (if the lacquer does not include an applicator)

Techniques

Rolling Simple Loops (page 17)

Using Jump Rings (page 16)

Note: You may not be able to find some of the exact charms shown in the featured piece. These are found objects that have caught the designer's eye. Use the descriptions—and look at the photo—for inspiration so that you can track down your own special finds.

Instructions

1. Spread the chain in front of you, and place the crystals, evenly spaced, along the length of the chain. To attach these, use the wire that connected each crystal to the chandelier. These wire pieces are ideal because each one already has a nice brad on the end. If you do not have the original wire (or are using new crystals), use head pins instead. Insert the wire or head pin, from front to back, through the top hole in the crystal. Trim the wire so it is just long enough to roll a loop over the end of the round-nose pliers. Once the simple loop is formed, the crystal can be attached to the chain using a jump ring.

2. Attach a miniature star to the hole in the bottom of each crystal, again using the original chandelier wire or a head pin (figure 1).

fig. 1

3. Cut a photo or image to fit inside each of the frame charms. Using the glue stick, attach the image to the frame. Cover the image with clear craft lacquer, letting the lacquer seep over the edges of the image and onto the metal surface.

4. Use jump rings to attach the charms to all of the links between the crystals.

5. Use a jump ring at each end of the chain to attach the parts of the toggle clasp.

Designer's Tips

Remove links from the leftover bracelet chain to make perfectly matched jump rings.

Do not shake the bottle of clear craft lacquer, as this will create bubbles you will not be able to remove when you coat your photos. Also, always let this lacquer dry completely, preferably overnight, before handling the piece.

You can never have too many charms!

SOUTHWEST

Sterling silver icons of the Southwest are interspersed with pieces of turquoise and arranged on a basic chain necklace.

Designer: Marlynn McNutt

Finished size: 18 inches (45.7 cm)

Materials

Turquoise nugget, 18 to 22 mm

Turquoise lentil, 10 mm

Sterling silver Kokopelli charm, 30 mm

Sterling silver axe charm, 33 mm

2 sterling silver Zuni bear beads, 13 mm

2 sterling silver feather charms, 31 mm

6 sterling silver jump rings, 6.5 mm

4 sterling silver head pins, 1½ inches
  (3.8 cm) long

Sterling silver lizard toggle clasp

18-inch length of 6 mm sterling silver
  ribbed flat cable chain

Tools

Chain-nose pliers, 2 pair

Round-nose pliers

Flush wire cutters

Techniques

Using Jump Rings (page 16)

Rolling Simple Loops (page 17)

Instructions

1. Open a jump ring, and slip it through the loop in the Kokopelli charm. Find the center link of the chain and close the jump ring around it, to attach the charm.

2. Using another jump ring, add the axe charm to the right of the Kokopelli charm.

3. Run a head pin up through one of the Zuni bears, and finish it with a simple loop. Twist open the loop you just made, thread it through one of the links to the right of the axe, and then close the loop.

4. Use a head pin and simple loop to make a dangle with the turquoise nugget (figure 1).

fig. 1

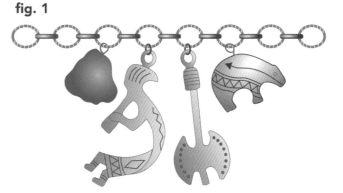

5. Thread the remaining Zuni bear and the turquoise lentil onto separate head pins, and the feather charms onto jump rings. Attach these elements to the left of the Kokopelli charm.

6. Using a jump ring, attach part of the toggle clasp to one end of the chain. Use the last jump ring to attach the last part of the toggle clasp to the opposite end of the chain.

Designer's Tip

A bead with a hollow body, such as the Zuni bears, might wobble too much when mounted on the head pin. You can control this by placing a small bead or spacer on the head pin before adding the bead. Make sure that the bead or spacer is small enough to slip up inside the hollow body so it is invisible.

TRINKETS

Every child lusts for these plastic geegaws at one time or another. Celebrate your inner child by fashioning them into a pair of amusing ear bobs.

Instructions

Instructions for Drops

Make two for each set.

1. Open the loop at the bottom of the ear wires.

2. Slide a charm onto each loop, and then securely close the loops (figure 1).

fig. 1

Instructions for Dangles

Make two.

1. Cut the chain in half. Set one piece aside for the second earring.

2. Open all of the jump rings, and slide a charm onto each one. Slip the last link of the chain onto one of the jump rings, and close it. Attach four more charms with jump rings, evenly spaced, along the length of the chain. Place the uppermost charm just a link or two from the top of the chain.

3. Slip another jump ring onto the top link of the embellished chain, and then through the loop at the bottom of the ear stud (figure 2).

fig. 2

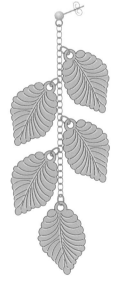

Designer: Terry Taylor

Finished size: Elephants or whistle and ball drops, 1½ inches (3.8 cm); leaf dangles, 3 inches (7.6 cm)

Materials

4 plastic charms, 19 mm

10 matching plastic charms, 19 mm

12 sterling silver jump rings, 6 mm

4 gold-filled French ear wires with bead

2 sterling silver ear studs (ball with drop), 6 mm

2½-inch (6.4 cm) length of 1.5 mm sterling silver chain

Tools

Chain-nose pliers, 2 pair

Round-nose pliers

Wire cutters

Techniques

Using Jump Rings (page 16)

FACES

Keep loved ones close at hand with charms that are a snap to make.

Instructions

Designer: Jean Campbell

Finished size: 7 inches (17.8 cm)

Materials

14 flat, smooth-face brass buttons with shanks, $^7/_{16}$ to $^5/_8$ inch (1.1 to 1.6 cm)

10 decorative buttons with shanks, $^7/_{16}$ to $^5/_8$ inch (1.1 to 1.6 cm)

Red, smoke, and white accent beads: glass pyramid, potato pearl, twisted hex, seed, bicone crystal, and druk, 3 to 6 mm

Sterling silver head pins, 2 inches (5 cm) long

Brass jump rings, 7 mm

2 brass jump rings, 5 mm

7-inch (17.8 cm) length of 8 mm heavy cable brass chain

Brass lobster clasp

14 small black-and-white photographs

Craft glue

Clear-coat acrylic sealer

Tools

Chain-nose pliers, 2 pair

Round-nose pliers

Pencil

Scissors

Craft mini-iron

Techniques

Using Jump Rings (page 16)

Rolling Simple Loops (page 17)

1. Match a photograph to one of the buttons for size. Make sure the image you would like captured is smaller than the face of the button. Center and trace a flat, smooth-face button onto the photograph. Cut the photograph inside the traced pencil line.

2. Carefully singe the edges of the photograph with the craft iron. Glue the photograph onto the button. After the glue is dry, cover the mounted photograph with sealer. Attach a 7 mm jump ring to the button's shank. Close the ring. Make 13 more photograph charms in the same manner.

3. Open a 5 mm jump ring and use it to attach one end of the chain to the lobster clasp. Close the ring. Attach the remaining part of the clasp to the opposite end of the chain using the last 5 mm jump ring.

4. Use the jump ring on each photograph charm to attach these items to the chain links at the desired points. Add a jump ring to each of the decorative buttons, and attach them to the chain.

5. String each accent bead onto a head pin. String some head pins with several beads, such as a combination of seed and twisted hex beads, to create larger dangles, finishing each with a wrapped loop. Using a jump ring, attach each of these dangles to the chain.

6. Place each pearl on a head pin, and secure the top with a wrapped loop to make a dangle. String three pearl dangles onto a jump ring and attach the ring to the chain (figure 1). Make and attach additional pearl-cluster dangles.

fig. 1

Designer's Tip

The clasp on this bracelet is intentionally small so it is hidden when the bracelet is worn.

ROCKER
CHIC

What delightful tidbits are scattered on your workbench? Gather them up and randomly stitch them to a cloth-covered bangle.

Instructions

Materials

5 bronze 11° seed beads

5 crystal bicones, 4 to 6 mm

4 brass or sterling silver charms, 4 to 8 mm

Small brass safety pins

4 jump rings (optional)

12-inch (30.5 cm) length of 24-gauge
   sterling wire

24-inch (61 cm) length of 2 mm curb chain

3 to 6-inch (7.6 to 15.2 cm) lengths of rolo,
   flat drawn, and curb chain; 1, 1.5, and
   2 mm links

Any kind of metal or sturdy plastic bangle,
   3 to 5 mm thick

Scrap of very soft silk or rayon velvet fabric

Size D nylon beading thread

Tools

Chain-nose pliers, 2 pair

Flat-nose pliers

Round-nose pliers

Flush wire cutters

Beading needle

Techniques

Using Jump Rings (page 16)

Overhand Knot (page 20)

Note: You may not be able to find some of the
exact charms shown in the featured piece. These
are found objects that have caught the designer's eye. Use the descriptions—and look at the
photo—for inspiration so that you can track
down your own special finds.

1. Cut the fabric scrap 2 inches (5 cm) wide and twice as long as the bangle's circumference. Twist and drape this piece over the bangle, and sew the lengthwise edges together so that the wrong side is not visible. Using the beading thread and the needle, sew the edges together with ladder stitches (figure 1).

fig. 1

2. Twist the fabric so that it is irregular and uneven. Make strategically placed small stitches with the thread and needle to permanently tack the random fabric folds as positioned.

3. Handling all of the scrap chain lengths as a single piece, tie an overhand knot around the bangle. Secure the knot with the sterling silver wire, making sure there are no ends sticking out to scratch the skin when the finished piece is worn. Cut the chain ends to random lengths.

4. Wrap some of the smaller curb chain around the bangle's circumference, letting some loops hang randomly. Tack the chain with small, random stitches made with the beading thread and needle. Continue sewing other short lengths of chain to the rest of the bangle's circumference.

5. Sew beads in some of the cracks and crevices of the fabric. Also thread a few seed beads onto some safety pins, and pin these to the fabric. Randomly pin other, empty safety pins to the fabric.

6. Sew charms to the bottom of the bracelet or use jump rings to add them to the chain loops. Balance the items on the piece for a random, yet balanced, appearance.

OUTRAGEOUS

Extravagant…over-the-top…Use the largest crystals and craziest charms you can find to give this eye-catching piece its extreme personality.

Instructions

Designer: Linda Larsen

Finished size: 7 inches (17.8 cm)

Materials

10 sterling silver rondelle spacers, 4 mm

5 faceted round crystals, 18 mm

3 vintage round sterling silver balls with set crystals, 18 mm

5 freshwater pearls (rice), 18 mm

7 sterling silver charms, 25 to 51 mm

10 sterling silver bead caps, 10 mm

22 sterling silver jump rings, 10 mm

Sterling silver toggle clasp

8 ball-end sterling silver head pins, 2½ inches (6.4 cm) long

16-inch (40.6 cm) length of 16-gauge sterling silver wire

6½-inch (16.5 cm) length of 13 mm sterling silver chain

Scraps of 2-mm chain to total 15 inches (38.1 cm)

Tools

Chain-nose pliers, 2 pair

Round-nose pliers

Flush wire cutters

Pencil

Techniques

Using Jump Rings (page 16)

Rolling Simple Loops (page 17)

Making Wrapped Loops (page 17)

Reaming Beads (page 18)

1. Connect all of the charms, evenly distributed, to links on the oversize chain, using a jump ring for each one.

2. Slide a rondelle spacer, crystal, and rondelle spacer onto a ball-end head pin. Make a wrapped loop above the upper rondelle spacer. Open a jump ring and slip the loop onto it, attach the crystal on the first link of the oversize chain, and close the jump ring. Assemble and attach the remaining crystal dangles in the same manner, evenly spacing them along the chain.

3. Thread each of the silver balls with set crystals onto a ball-end head pin, and make a simple loop at the top (wrapping the wire twice around the tip of the round-nose pliers). Attach these dangles to the oversize chain using jump rings.

4. Cut three lengths of tiny chain: 1¼, 1, and ¾ inches (3.2, 2.5, and 1.9 cm). Cut a 3-inch (7.6 cm) length of wire. Make a simple loop at one end, using the round-nose pliers. Open it with the chain-nose pliers, add the end link of each piece of small chain, and then close the loop. Add a bead cap, a freshwater pearl, and another bead cap to the wire. Finish the top of the dangle with a wrapped loop. (You may have to ream out the pearl to get the wire through.) Make four more pearl dangles in the same manner.

5. Attach all of the pearl dangles to the oversize chain with jump rings, as shown in figure 1.

fig. 1

6. Attach the parts of the toggle clasp to the ends of the oversize chain, using jump rings.

FLOWER POWER

Roll some loops, stitch a few seed beads, attach some dangles,
and you're ready to channel some vibrant energy.

Designer: Candie Cooper

Finished size: To fit the purchased bracelet

Materials

4 turquoise plastic flower spacer beads,
   10 mm

6 orange plastic flower spacer beads,
   10 mm

16 multicolor 8° seed beads

2 white felt balls with beads, 12 mm

2 red flower spacer beads, 12 mm

2 turquoise swirl glass beads, 8 mm

Orange polka-dot bead, 12 mm

2 brass bird charms, 12 mm

4 green glass leaf charms, 13 mm

5 bright color felt flowers, ¾ inch
   (1.9 cm) thick

4 silver plated jump rings, 6 mm

4 silver plated jump rings, 5 mm

5 silver plated head pins, 2 inches
   (5 cm) long

3 silver plated eye pins, 2 inches
   (5 cm) long

6-inch (15.2 cm) length of 18-gauge silver
   plated wire

Silver plated 9 mm bracelet with clasp

Craft glue

Sewing thread to match felt flowers

(Continued on next page)

Instructions

1. Glue one turquoise plastic flower bead to the center of each side of the blue felt flower. Attach turquoise and orange plastic flower beads to both sides of the remaining felt flowers.

2. With thread on the hand-sewing needle, anchor the end with a few stitches through the center of one of the felt flowers. String one seed bead onto the needle. Pull the needle and thread down through the center of a plastic flower and out through the opposite side (bottom) of the felt flower. String another seed bead onto the needle, and pull the needle and thread back through the center of the felt flower. Don't pull through the plastic flower and bead on top. Make several small stitches in the middle of the flower center and then trim off the thread ends. Repeat this step for the remaining felt flowers.

3. Cut the tip of one of the head pins at an angle and poke it through the felt flower (figure 1). Roll a simple loop at the top of the head pin using the round-nose pliers. Complete all of the felt flower charms in the same manner.

fig. 1

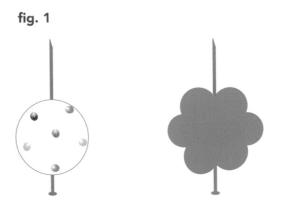

4. Attach a bird charm to the loop of an eye pin. Cut the tip of the eye pin at an angle. String one seed bead, felt ball, and seed bead onto the pin. Finish the end of the wire with a simple loop, taking care not to squish the ball when you bend the eye pin. Make another bird dangle in the same way.

Tools

Chain-nose pliers, 2 pair

Flat-nose pliers

Round-nose pliers

Wire cutters

Hand-sewing needle

Scissors

Techniques

Using Jump Rings (page 16)

Rolling Simple Loops (page 17)

5. Make a loop at one end of the wire.
String a red flower spacer bead onto
the wire, followed by a clear and
turquoise swirl glass bead and finish it
with a simple loop (figure 2). Position
the two loops perpendicular to each other
by grasping one loop with the flat-nose pliers and the
other with the chain-nose pliers and twisting them into
place. Repeat this step to make a second flower link.

fig. 2

6. Remove the clasp from the bracelet. Add the length of
the chain plus the lengths of the two flower links and
the clasp. Compare this to the length you want your
bracelet to be, and remove chain links, if necessary (see
Personalizing Fit, page 20). Open the loop at the bottom of the flower bead link and connect it to one end
of the chain. Attach the remaining flower link to the
opposite end of the chain. Connect the clasp to a
remaining loop on either of the flower bead links.

7. String a seed bead, the polka-dot bead, and a seed
bead onto an eye pin, and finish the pin with a simple loop. Use the bottom loop to connect a felt flower
charm. Use the top loop to connect the dangle to the
center link of the bracelet.

8. Spread the bracelet horizontally in front of you. Lay
the remaining charms out so they are evenly spaced.
Attach them along the chain, using 6 mm jump rings
for the leaf charms, and 5 mm jump rings for the
flower charms. Attach the felt ball dangles with the
loop at the top.

PENNIES FROM HEAVEN

The designer of this bracelet searches for souvenir penny machines everywhere he travels. These charming machines (no pun intended) flatten and imprint a penny with a specially engraved die.

Designer: Terry Taylor

Finished size: 8 inches (20.3 cm)

Materials

10 teardrop beads, 13 mm

15 flat souvenir pennies

10 head pins, 2 inches (5 cm) long

17 copper jump rings, 5 mm

Copper toggle clasp

15-inch (38.1 cm) length of 5 mm copper link chain

1 teaspoon of salt

¼ cup white vinegar

Tools

Chain-nose pliers, 2 pair

Needle-nose pliers

Wire cutters

Rawhide mallet

Shallow glass bowl

Hand towel

Awl or nail with a flat head

Safety glasses

Drill and 1/16-inch (1.6 mm) drill bit

Half-round file

Techniques

Using Jump Rings (page 16)

Making Wrapped Loops (page 17)

Drilling Holes in Metal (page 19)

Instructions

1. Souvenir pennies may be slightly curved when they come out of the machine. If this is the case, place them on a sturdy work surface, one at a time, and tap on them with a rawhide mallet to flatten them.

2. Pour the salt and vinegar into the bowl. Stir the mix until the salt is dissolved. Place the pennies in the bowl to soak for about 5 minutes. When removed, wipe the pennies with a hand towel to reveal the shiny surface.

3. Use an awl or nail to make a divot at the top of the penny, where you wish to drill a hole (figure 1). Use a small drill bit to create a hole in each penny. Smooth the edges with the file.

fig. 1

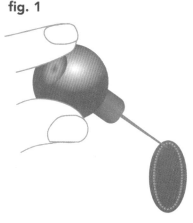

4. Cut the chain into two equal lengths. Spread both pieces in front of you. Plan the finished position of the pennies and beads by placing them underneath the chains. Leave these items in position as you work through the next few steps.

5. Attach pennies to the chain links of both lengths of chain, using a jump ring for each penny.

Designer's Tips

You can purchase flattened pennies online, but that's not as much fun as finding the machine and imprinting your own. You can find them everywhere except in federally owned venues. Why? It's illegal to deface or alter currency for fraudulent purposes. Don't worry, the government won't chase after you when you wear your finished bracelet, because you can't use these pennies in the gum machine, and no cashier will accept them!

If you don't have a rawhide mallet, sandwich a penny between two pieces of scrap wood and flatten the penny with a regular hammer.

6. Slide a bead onto a head pin. Roll the head pin to create a loop. Slide the wire through a chain link (figure 2). Wrap the end of the wire around the head pin that is coming out the top of the bead. Cut off the excess wire. Attach all of the remaining beads to both chain lengths in the same manner.

fig. 2

7. Open a jump ring and slip on part of the toggle clasp and the last link of one end of each chain. Close the jump ring. Use another jump ring to attach the remaining toggle clasp part and the opposite ends of the chains.

INTERMEDIATE PROJECTS

MEMENTOS

Extend earrings to
new lengths with a link
made from another charm.

Instructions

Designer: Andrea Trbovich

Finished size: 2½ inches (6.4 cm)

Materials

2 stamps in photo charms, 24 mm

2 sterling silver imitation subway tokens, 18 mm

2 French ear wires with wire wrap and ball

2 sterling silver jump rings, 3.5 mm

Tools

Chain-nose pliers, 2 pair

Flat-nose pliers

Safety glasses

Drill and 1/16-inch (1.6 mm) drill bit

Round needle file

Techniques

Using Jump Rings (page 16)

Drilling Holes in Metal (page 19)

1. Make a divot at the top and bottom of the subway token by making a quick twist with the tip of the drill bit at the desired spots. Silver is soft enough to indent easily. Place the bit in the drill, and make a hole at each divot. File the rough edges around the holes.

2. Use the two chain-nose pliers to grip the sides of a jump ring. Twist the sides apart to open it. Thread the stamp charm and bottom hole of the subway token charm onto the jump ring (figure 1). Close the ring securely.

fig. 1

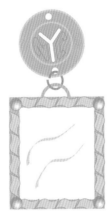

3. Using flat-nose pliers, twist open the loop at the bottom of the ear wire. Thread the top of the subway token onto the open loop. Twist the loop to close it.

Designer's Tip

Be sure to stay well within the border on the subway token when drilling. If the hole is too close to the edge, it will compromise the structural integrity of the charm.

ECLECTIC

You can quickly pull together a chic fashion-forward look by knotting ribbons around simple dangles.

Finished size: 2½ inches (6.4 cm)

Materials

Black iridescent bead (flat diamond), 5 mm

Black glass bead with white polka dots, 12 mm

Silver hat charm, 3.8 cm

Pink plastic heart charm, 10 mm

Ceramic pear charm, 15 mm

3 silver plated jump rings, 5 mm

Silver plated eye pin, 2 inches (5 cm) long

Silver plated stick pin with loop, 2½ inches (6.4 cm) long

1-inch (2.5 cm) length of 4 mm silver plated chain

5-inch (12.7 cm) length of black-and-white stripped ribbon, ⅜ inch (9.5 mm) wide

5-inch (12. 7 cm) length of green ribbon with white dots, ³⁄₁₆ inch (5 mm) wide

Craft glue with precision applicator

Tools

Chain-nose pliers, 2 pair

Round-nose pliers

Wire cutters

Scissors

Techniques

Using Jump Rings (page 16)

Rolling Simple Loops (page 17)

Overhand Knot (page 20)

Instructions

1. Connect the hat charm to one end of the chain with a jump ring, using the two chain-nose pliers. Open the loop on the eye pin, connect the heart charm, and close the loop. String the small black bead onto the eye pin, and finish with a simple loop rolled on the round-nose pliers. Slip the simple loop onto the second to the last link of the chain, just above the hat charm. Close the loop.

2. Connect the pear charm four links above the heart dangle, using a jump ring. Use another jump ring to attach the end of the chain to the loop on the stick pin.

3. Place the green ribbon on top of the striped ribbon and, handling the ribbons as a single layer, tie a loose, overhand knot. Remove the cap on the stick pin, and thread the pointed end through the overhand knot. Slide the knot up the pin until it is next to the jump ring. Tighten the knot, and use scissors to trim the ribbon tails at an angle.

4. Add a drop of glue to the stick pin just below the ribbon. Slide the black polka-dot bead up the stick pin until it is next to the ribbon (figure 1).

fig. 1

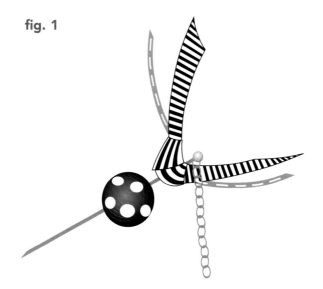

SPRINGTIME

Rejuvenate vintage jewelry with crystals and glass beads.

Instructions

Designer: Candie Cooper

Finished size: Bird 3 inches (7.6 cm);
    flower, 3 inches (7.6 cm)

Swallow Materials

3 blue glass beads, 6 mm

Brass nest charm, 25 mm

Brass treble clef charm, 12 mm

Music note charm, 8 mm

Bird brooch, 2 inches (5 cm)

6 brass bead caps, 5 mm

4 gold-color jump rings, 5 mm

3 gold-color eye pins, 2 inches (5 cm) long

Tie tack

1-inch (2.5 cm) length of 4 mm old
    brass chain

Craft glue with precision applicator

Flower Materials

2 AB crystal beads (round), 8 mm

Pink glass pearl bead (round), 6 mm

Brass leaf charm, 15 mm

2 brass bell bead caps to fit the crystals

2 brass bead caps, 5 mm

Flower brooch, 1¼ inches (3.2 cm)

2 gold-color jump rings, 5 mm

2 gold-color head pins, 2 inches (5 cm) long

1 gold-color eye pin, 2 inches (5 cm) long

(Continued on page 60)

Swallow Instructions

1. Scratch up the flat back of the tie tack finding by rubbing it with the coarse sandpaper. Place a dot of glue on the back of the nest charm, and push the flat side of the tie tack into the glue. Make sure that some of the adhesive comes up around the edge of the finding.

2. String a bead cap, blue bead, and bead cap onto an eye pin, and roll a simple loop at the top, using the tip of the round-nose pliers. Make two more dangles in the same manner. Remove one link from the chain, and use it to connect blue bead pieces (figure 1). Connect the last blue bead piece to complete the beaded chain.

fig. 1

3. The oil from your hands might tarnish the new metal charms, so that they are more compatible with the look of the older pieces. Create a slightly distressed look by rubbing the charms with fine sandpaper.

Tools

Chain-nose pliers, 2 pair

Flat-nose pliers

Round-nose pliers

Wire cutters

Coarse and fine sandpaper

Techniques

Using Jump Rings (page 16)

Rolling Simple Loops (page 17)

Designer's Tips

To bring new life to old brooches, use links from old chains to connect charms and bead dangles. This way, the metals match.

Look for brooches with holes that can be used for jump rings wherever you want to attach charms.

Select beads to match stones in the brooch, so they blend together.

Select a brooch with a theme for which you can find charms easily.

4. Open a jump ring, slide the treble clef charm onto it, and then insert the ring through a brass chain link on the beaded chain. Close the jump ring so it is secure. Attach the music note charm to another brass link in the same manner.

5. Open a jump ring, and connect the end of the beaded chain closest to the treble clef to the bird brooch by closing the jump ring around the tail. Open the remaining jump ring, and connect the loose end of the beaded chain to the nest charm.

Flower Instructions

1. String a crystal bead and bell bead cap onto a head pin, and finish the end of the wire with a loop. Make a second crystal bead dangle in the same manner.

2. String a bead cap, pink glass pearl bead, and bead cap onto the eye pin, and finish with a loop. Open the loop on the eye pin, and connect the leaf charm (figure 2).

fig. 2

3. Open the loop at the top of the leaf dangle and connect it to the center bottom of the flower brooch. Connect the crystal dangles at each side, using the gold jump rings.

FIESTA

String a joyful medley of colors and shapes with a simple, easy process.

FIESTA

Designer: Bonnie Clewans

Finished size: 51 inches (129.5 cm)

Materials

7 opaque turquoise bicone crystals, 4 mm

Millefiore glass tube bead, 15 mm

Golden horn bead (round), 10 mm

Coral bicone bead (cushion), 15 mm

Black, side-drill horn bead (donut), 20 mm

Faceted gold stone (rondelle), 4 mm

5 grams of 11° multicolor opaque
    seed beads

Chevron bead, 30 mm

10 grams of 8° multicolor opaque
    seed beads

20 sterling silver rondelle spacers, 4 mm

12 turquoise nuggets, 4 to 12 mm

2 sterling silver coin charms, 10 mm

4 sterling silver head pins, 2 inches
    (5 cm) long

6 sterling silver crimp beads, 1.5 mm

2 sterling silver pronged bead caps, 14 mm

4 sterling silver crimp tubes, 2 mm

Sterling silver spring ring clasp with
    soldered rings

4-yard (3.6 m) length of .010 nylon-coated
    beading wire

(Continued on next page)

Instructions

1. Thread a turquoise bicone, the millefiore bead, and a turquoise bicone onto a head pin. Finish the top with a wrapped loop. Make two more bead drops in the same manner, one featuring the golden horn bead in the center and the other using the coral cushion. The final bead dangle starts by threading the black horn bead on a head pin, followed by the faceted gold stone rondelle, and then a turquoise bicone. Finish the top of the head pin with a wrapped loop.

2. Cut the beading wire into 24-inch (61 cm) lengths. On the first piece, string a crimp bead and a bead dangle. Turn the beading wire, and thread it through the same crimp bead. Squeeze the crimp bead closed. Trim off the excess wire. In the same manner, attach a bead drop to one end of three more wire lengths.

3. Thread a crimp bead onto a new length of beading wire, add four 11° seed beads, a coin charm, and four more seed beads; turn the wire, and feed it through the crimp bead you added first. Squeeze the crimp (figure 1). Trim off the excess wire. Attach the remaining charm to another length of beading wire in the same manner.

fig. 1

crimp
beed

4. On each piece of beading wire, add 2 to 3 inches (5 to 7.6 cm) of 11° beads to form fringes of varying lengths for a tassel.

Designer's Tips

Make sure that the bead caps fit the ends of the chevron bead, and that this large bead has a 2 mm hole.

Frequently, nuggets come in a variety of sizes on a single strand. Use the larger ones at the bottom and middle of the beading wires, and smaller ones at the top.

Consider using Czech beads for this project, because they are sold in strands or hanks. It is very easy to take the beads off the hank with the wire, so stringing will be a breeze.

Techniques

Making Wrapped Loops (page 17)

Reaming Beads (page 18)

Using Crimp Beads and Tubes (page 19)

5. Thread all six strands through a bead cap, the large chevron, and a bead cap. At the top, separate three strands of wire for each side of the necklace.

6. Working on one side of the necklace, with three strands of wire held together, string 8° seed beads until the beaded strand is 1¾ inches (4.4 cm) from the top of the bead cap on top of the chevron (figure 2). Add a rondelle spacer, turquoise nugget, and rondelle spacer. Continue adding beads in the same order and amount until all six nuggets are strung. When adding the last nugget, do not include a rondelle spacer on either side. Also, make sure the last nugget has a hole large enough to hold six strands of wire. (If necessary, ream the bead.)

fig. 2

7. Thread two crimp tubes and part of the clasp onto the wire, turn the wire, and thread it back through the crimp tubes and the last nugget. Snug the wire so no spaces are visible. Crimp the tubes, and trim off the excess wire.

8. Complete the opposite side of the necklace in the same manner.

GRAMMY'S BAUBLES

Rhinestones! Crystals! Beads! Flowers! This piece has it all. An over-the-top chunky charm bracelet makes the most of vintage earrings and brooches.

Instructions

Designer: Andrea Trbovich

Finished size: 7 inches (17.8 cm)

Materials

4 sets of vintage earrings, 20 mm

Vintage brooch, 35 mm

6 vintage charms, 5 to 15 mm

15 silver-color jump rings, 10 mm

7-inch (17.8 cm) length of 8 mm silver-color link chain

8-inch (20.3 cm) length of gold-color 10 mm crystal link chain necklace with clasp

Tools

Chain-nose pliers, 2 pair

Flat-nose pliers

Wire cutters

Safety glasses

Drill and .74 to 1.61-mm drill bit

Flat file

Techniques

Using Jump Rings (page 16)

Drilling Holes in Metal (page 19)

Designer's Tip

The metal for the findings, chain, and vintage pieces don't need to match. It is more important that all of the pieces share a theme. For this bracelet, all of the pieces convey the impression of a flower and include at least some blue.

1. Using the wire cutters, carefully remove the earring clips and pin backs from the jewelry pieces. Smooth any rough edges with the file.

2. Pick out the pieces that have filigree, holes, or wiring that you can use to attach a jump ring. Open a jump ring and slip it through a hole—or underneath a secure piece of wire—on an earring or brooch (figures 1 and 2). Twist the jump ring to close it. Add a jump ring to each of the selected pieces and charms in the same manner.

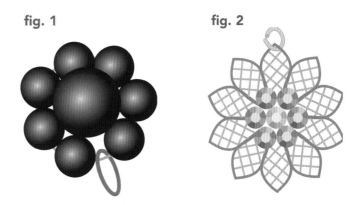

fig. 1

fig. 2

3. Gather the remaining jewelry pieces. Drill a hole near the top of each one, through metal only (figure 3). Be cautious you do not shift the arrangement of any beads, crystals, or rhinestones as you drill and wire each piece. If there is not an area that can easily accommodate drilling, choose a position where one small bead or rhinestone could be removed easily without a noticeable loss. Often, a rhinestone will pop out when you start drilling on the back, directly behind the position where the rhinestone is set. File off all of the rough edges, and then insert a jump ring through the hole.

fig. 3

4. Spread the silver-color chain in front of you, and arrange the charms in the manner you would like to attach them. Place the largest piece in the middle. For symmetry, position one piece of each earring set on either side of the center. Use the jump rings to attach the pieces as arranged.

5. Cut the crystal chain to match the bracelet length. Do not cut off the end with the clasp. Open the last link at both ends of the silver-color chain, and close them around the last links of the crystal chain.

OLDE WORLD

The elegance of pearls and jade complement
and contrast with sleek metal disks.

OLDE WORLD

Designer: Marie Lee Carter

Finished size: 20 inches (50.8 cm)

Materials

20 pearls (rounds or rondelles), 4mm

2 jade beads, 4 mm

20 sterling silver jump rings, 3 mm

Sterling silver clasp

48-inch (121.9 cm) length of 22-gauge
   sterling silver wire (dead soft, round)

18-inch (45.7 cm) length of sterling silver
   4 mm cable chain

6 x 1-inch (15.2 x 2.5 cm) piece of
   16-gauge sterling silver sheet metal

(Continued on next page)

Instructions

1. Using a scribe, mark 3 circles, each ½ inch (1.3 cm), and 2 ovals, each ¼ x 9/16 inch (6 mm x 1.4 cm), on the sterling silver sheet. Cut out the shapes with the saw. Use the files to smooth all of the edges.

2. Using the felt marker, mark three holes at the bottom of each circle and one at the top. Mark one hole at the bottom of each oval and one at the top. Make an indentation with the center punch before drilling. Put on the safety glasses and carefully drill the holes. Check circles and ovals for uniformity, and clean up any areas with the sandpaper, using the coarse, and then the fine, grit sandpaper.

3. Cut a 2-inch (5 cm) length of wire for each pearl and bead. To create a pearl drop, roll a small simple loop at one end of a piece of cut wire. Hammer the loop—just once—with the ball peen hammer. Thread on a pearl. Make a 90° degree bend in the wire, above the pearl, and then roll the wire twice around the tip of the round-nose pliers to create a double loop (figure 1). Use the flat-nose pliers to hold the double loop while you wrap the end of the wire three times around the base to close the loop. Snip off the excess wire, and file the end.

fig. 1

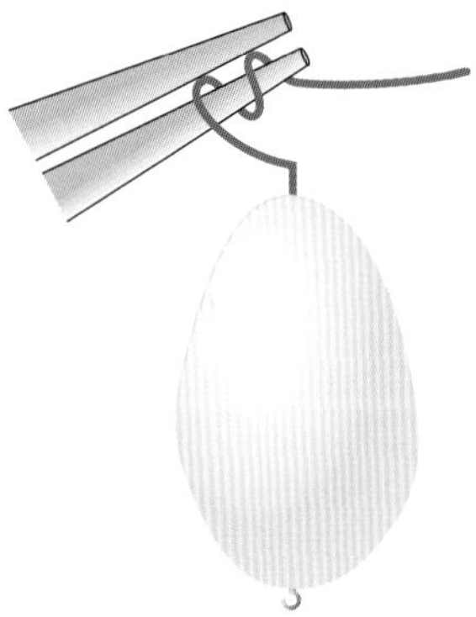

Designer's Tips

If you do not want to ream any beads or pearls, buy your supplies in person so you can make sure that the holes can accommodate the 24-gauge round wire.

The disks can be made with sterling silver sheet of any gauge between 14 and 22. A clasp can be attached before you start adding beads and dangles, or at the very end of the process. Unless there are special materials or techniques, you can apply the clasp whenever you want. To give your creative process closure, you might want the clasp to be the last thing you do.

4. Make a triangular wrap using another piece of cut wire and a round bead (figure 2). Snip off the excess wire and file the end.

fig. 2

5. Attach jump rings to each of the drill holes that you made in the bottoms of the circles and ovals. Before closing each jump ring, attach one pearl drop.

6. Use one jump ring to attach the top of each circle and oval to the chain. Before closing each jump ring, attach one pearl drop to the front of each circle and attach a bead to the front of each oval. At both ends of the disk arrangement, attach three pearl drops using a jump ring.

7. Use jump rings to attach the clasp to the chain.

8. Tumble for 20 to 40 minutes, if desired.

Tools

Chain-nose pliers, 2 pair

Flat-nose pliers

Round-nose pliers

Flush wire cutters

Scribe

Jeweler's saw and blade

Fine-tip permanent pen

Barrette file

Half-round file

Center punch

Safety glasses

Drill and small drill bit

400- and 600-grit sandpaper

Ball peen hammer

Tumbler, stainless steel shot, plastic pellets, and detergent (optional)

Techniques

Using Jump Rings (page 16)

Rolling Simple Loops (page 17)

Making Wrapped Loops (page 17)

Reaming Beads (page 18)

DIVINE

Showcase exquisite padparadschas (the rarest naturally occurring colored crystal) and beautiful polygon crystals in these sweet earrings.

Instructions

Make two Angels and two Crystal Bows.

1. For an Angel earring, thread a polygon crystal, angel wings, pearl, rondelle, and bicone onto a head pin (figure 1). For a crystal bow earring, thread a cube onto a head pin.

2. Finish the dangle with a wrapped head pin. Use the crimp tool to tuck in any excess wire, taking care not to crush the top bead.

3. This step is only for the crystal bow earring. Cut the wire into two 4-inch (10.2 cm) lengths. Set one piece of wire aside to make the matching earring. Position the round-nose pliers 1½ inches (3.8 cm) from the top of the remaining piece of wire. Holding the wire below the pliers, bend the wire away from you to make a right angle. Pull the wire over the top of the nose of the pliers. Remove the pliers. Thread the wire-wrapped cube onto the loop. Holding the open loop tightly with the round-nose pliers, wrap the short end of the wire around the long end three times. Trim off the excess wire on the short end only. Thread the bow and round crystal onto the wire (figure 2). Make a wrapped loop above the crystal.

4. Carefully open the loop on the ear wire, slip on the dangle, and close the ear wire loop.

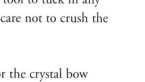

fig. 1

fig. 2

Designer's Tip

You can paint the angel wings with nail polish or enamel model paint if you want to add more interest.

Designer: Bonnie Clewans

Finished sizes: Angel earrings, 1¾ inches (4.4 cm); Crystal Bow earrings 1⅝ inches (4.1 cm)

Angel Materials

2 crystals (polygon), 12 mm

2 pearls (round), 6 mm

2 rhinestone rondelles, 5 mm

2 bicone crystals, 3 mm

2 gold plated pewter angel wings, 8 mm

2 gold filled head pins, 2 inches (5 cm) long

2 lever back ear wires

Crystal Bow Materials

2 padparadscha crystals (cube), 8 mm

2 faceted crystals (round), 3 mm

2 silver plated pewter bows, 10 mm

2 sterling silver head pins, 2 inches (5 cm) long

2 lever back, gold filled ear wires

8-inch (20.3 cm) length of 24-gauge half-hard sterling silver wire

Tools

Round-nose pliers

Fine wire cutters

Crimp tool

Ruler

Glue

Techniques

Making Wrapped Loops (page 17)

SUNSET

Adding a beaded slide gives a thick cord or braid an entirely new look.

Instructions

1. Cut one length of memory wire that has four complete coils. Make a small loop at one end of the wire using the round-nose pliers.

2. From the opposite end of the wire, slide enough 6° seed beads to the eye to cover one complete loop (figure 1). String a 1-inch (2.5 cm) length of chain onto the memory wire, and snug it up against the closest seed bead. Continue adding seed beads, inserting another length of chain at every complete circle, until you reach the end. This slide has a total of five pieces of chain. From right to left, they measure 1, 1¼, 1½, ¾, and 1 inch (2.5, 3.2, 3.8, 1.9, and 2.5 cm). Before stringing the fifth length of chain, make a simple loop at the end of the wire. Thread the chain onto this loop (figure 2)

Designer: Gloria Farver

Finished size: To fit your purchased necklace

Materials

Tube of 6° seed beads in colors to match necklace

Tube of 11° metallic silver seed beads

8 bicone crystals, 3 mm

2 silver-color rondelle spacers, 3 mm

Metallic silver bead, 4 mm

Metallic silver tube bead, 2 mm

3 sterling silver beads (assorted shapes), 6 to 10 mm

2 word charms with loops, 6 mm

13 head pins, 2 inches (5 cm) long

Memory wire, ring size

6-inch (15.2 cm) length of 22-gauge sterling silver wire

5½-inch (14 cm) length of sterling silver 5 mm link chain

Thick cord necklace with clasp

Tools

Round-nose pliers

Wire cutters

Memory wire shears

Techniques

Rolling Simple Loops (page 17)

Making Wrapped Loops (page 17)

fig. 1   **fig. 2**

3. On a head pin, stack a metallic seed bead, a bicone, and a metallic seed bead. Make a wrapped loop with the top of the head pin, attaching it to a link near the top of the first chain on the right. Stack combinations of beads on head pins to make 9 more dangles, attaching each one to a link along any of the chain lengths as you finish the wrap at the top of the head pin.

4. Cut a 3-inch (7.6 cm) length of wire, and make a wrapped loop at one end, threading a word charm onto the wire before finishing the wrap. Thread a silver seed bead, bicone, and a silver seed bead. Finish the link with a wrapped loop at the top while attaching it to the bottom link of a chain. Make and attach another word charm.

5. Thread metallic seed beads and large beads onto head pins, and attach these to the last link of the remaining chains while wrapping the loop on the head pin.

WHIRLPOOL

Roll silver wire into spirals and curves that link
and swirl around focal beads.

Instructions

Designer: Tamara Honaman

Finished size: 8¾ inches (22.2 cm)

Materials

Focal bead, 20 mm

6 sterling silver beads (round), 3 mm

12 sterling silver rondelle spacers, 5 mm

4 lampwork glass beads, 8 to 10 mm

2 sterling silver charms, 10 to 15 mm

13 sterling silver jump rings, 6 to 10 mm

6 sterling silver ball-end head pins,
    2½ inches (6.4 cm) long

34½-inch (87.6 cm) length of 14-gauge
    sterling silver wire

24-inch (61 cm) length of 24-gauge
    sterling silver wire

Tools

Chain-nose pliers, 2 pair

Flat-nose pliers

Round-nose pliers

Heavy-duty flush wire cutters

Tape measure

Ball peen hammer

Techniques

Making Wrapped Loops (page 17)

1. Cut a 3-inch (7.6 cm) piece of 14-gauge wire with a blunt cut at both ends. Slightly flatten each end with a hammer. Grip the tip of the wire in the round-nose pliers. Rotate your wrist away from your body, to form a ⅛ to ³⁄₁₆-inch (3 to 5 mm) eye at the end of the wire. Rotate the piece and make an eye at the other end, in the opposite direction.

2. Place the wire in the jaws of the round-nose pliers, near the hinge. Rest one eye just above the plier's barrel, and pivot, with the eye coming up, toward you. Rotate the pliers away from you to form a shepherd's hook. Repeat this motion at the opposite end of the wire to complete an S-link. Link a jump ring through both eyes. Make two more S-links.

3. Cut a 5-inch (12.7 cm) piece of 14-gauge wire with a blunt cut at both ends. Slightly flatten both ends with a hammer. Use the round-nose pliers to make an eye at the tip of the wire. Grip the eye and rotate your wrist again, wrapping the wire to start the second layer of the spiral.

4. Grip the growing spiral, flat in the flat-nose pliers, and lay wire down around the previous layer. Build the spiral—moving the wire while holding the pliers in one position—until 1 to 1½ inches (2.5 to 3.8 cm) of wire remain. Form a new eye at the end of the remaining wire. Grip the large spiral with the flat-nose pliers, grip the smaller loop with the chain-nose pliers, and then flip the smaller loop so it is vertical to the larger spiral. Change your grip on the eye and then continue wrapping the wire to start the second layer of a new spiral (figure 1).

fig. 1

5. Blunt-cut a 6-inch (15.2 cm) length of 14-gauge wire. Slightly flatten the ends. Make an eye at one end of the wire, and make a spiral no more than two revolutions deep. Tightly wrap the 24-gauge wire around 4 inches (10.2 cm) of the 14-gauge wire, and slide this up to the base of the small spiral, working the coil into the spiral so the coil is caught or stabilized. Trim any excess wire. Continue making the spiral, incorporating the coil, until you have 1 inch (2.5 cm) of 14-gauge wire remaining. Make a new eye, in the opposite direction to the first spiral, at the remaining end of the 14-gauge wire. Continue to spiral the wire until it meets the previous spiral.

6. Blunt-cut a 4½-inch (11.4 cm) piece of 14-gauge wire. Make an eye at one end, and then work a spiral until 2 inches (5 cm) remain. Using the round-nose pliers, grip the wire above the spiral. Bend the remaining length of wire around one barrel of the pliers to form the neck of the clasp (figure 2). Grip the tip of the wire, and form an eye to finish the end of the swan clasp. With the hammer, slightly flatten the curve of the neck.

fig. 2

7. To start the first half of the focal bead cage, measure the outside of the focal bead, from hole to hole. Add 4 inches (10.2 cm). Cut a piece of the 14-gauge wire to this final measurement. Blunt-cut both ends of the wire. Shape the wire into a spiral at one end that is large enough to span the hole of the focal bead.

8. Place the spiral over a hole on the focal bead. Bend the wire over the bead, to the hole on the other side. The amount of wire past the hole should be just enough to make a spiral. Create the second spiral, curling it in the opposite direction.

9. Place the spiral piece of the cage around the focal bead. Blunt-cut a 4-inch (10.2 cm) length of 14-gauge wire. Insert the wire through the hole in the center of one spiral, through the focal bead, and out the center of the second spiral. Center the focal bead on the wire.

10. Bend the wire to cross at one end of the bead. Make spirals at each end of the wire until the holes meet. Keep the spirals loose enough to allow enough space for the focal bead to move smoothly.

11. Add a rondelle spacer, lampwork glass bead, rondelle spacer, and small round bead onto a head pin. Make a wrapped loop just above the stacked items, threading the dangle onto the last jump ring in the linked items. Make five more dangles, using the beads, charms, and head pins. Slip two dangles onto one curve of two of the S-shaped wire pieces.

12. Making sure that the finished piece is relatively flat so it can rest horizontally on a flat surface, link the elements together, using jump rings as needed (figure 3). Attach the remaining dangles to jump rings that have been used to link the shaped wire pieces. Attach the swan clasp to one end.

fig. 3

TALISMAN

Repetition of shapes unifies a quirky assortment of metal plates and found objects.

Instructions

Designer: Susan Lenart Kazmer

Finished size: 7 inches (17.8 cm)

Materials

Dark-color beads, 5 to 8 mm

Tube of dark-color 11° seed beads

Brass, copper, sterling silver, or stainless steel rectangular found objects, 10 x 25 mm to 9 x 40 mm

Brass, copper, and stainless steel circular found objects, 10 to 30 mm

22-gauge sterling silver sheet metal

Jump rings in various metals, 5 to 8 mm

Ball-end sterling silver head pins, 2 inches (5 cm) long

Sterling silver eye pins, 2 inches (5 cm) long

Sterling silver clasp

24-gauge base metal wire

16-gauge annealed steel wire

6½-inch (16.5 cm) length of 6 mm base metal chain

Antiquing, liver of sulphur, or patina solution

Matte medium

Paper printed with images and words, to fit the found objects

Thin sheet of mica or clear, hard plastic

Note: You may not be able to find some of the exact charms shown in the featured piece. These are found objects that have caught the designer's eye. Use the descriptions—and look at the photos—for inspiration so that you can track down your own special finds.

(Continued on page 80)

1. Cut the sheet metal into rectangles ranging from ⅜ to ⅝ inch (9.5 mm to 1.6 cm) wide and 1 to 2 inches (2.5 to 5 cm) long. Cut several pairs to the same size. Use the metal file to clean up and smooth the edges by pushing the file away from you. Oxidize or apply the antiquing or patina solution to the rectangles. Glue very small scraps of paper to some of the pieces with the matte medium. Set aside the matching rectangles for use in step 2.

2. Select two scraps of paper to showcase between two matching pieces of flat metal. Draw a rectangle with a fine-tip permanent marker where you want to cut out a window that will allow you to see the paper inside when the riveting is finished. Drill a hole in a corner of the window. Insert the blade of the jeweler's saw into the hole and fix the other end into the saw. Saw along the drawn lines until the center falls out. Use the metal file to clean up and smooth the edges by pushing the file away from you. Make a matching window in the other piece of metal.

3. Cut two pieces of mica or clear, hard plastic, both slightly larger than the window. Place the mica under each window, with a paper image on top.

4. Stack all the layers (silver sheet metal, mica, paper image (face down), paper image (faceup), mica, and silver sheet metal) with the metal edges aligned (figure 1). Place the stack in a small clamp. Drill straight through all the layers at a corner.

fig. 1

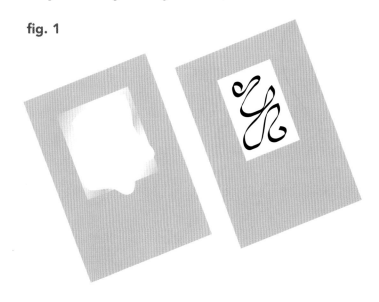

Tools

Chain-nose pliers, 2 pair

Flat-nose pliers

Round-nose pliers

Flush wire cutters

Metal file

Fine-tip permanent marker

Jeweler's saw and blade

Small clamp

Safety glasses

Drill and 1/16-inch (1.6 mm) drill bit

Anvil

Small ball peen hammer

Small paintbrush

Techniques

Using Jump Rings (page 16)

Rolling Simple Loops (page 17)

Making Wrapped Loops (page 17)

Making Triangular Wraps (page 18)

Designer's Tip

Rivets are the strongest method of attaching metal to metal besides soldering. For a piece that has unusual materials, such as wood, paper, and plastic, you don't have the option of soldering since these materials wouldn't survive the heat.

5. Place the stack on an anvil. Insert the annealed wire, that has been filed, all the way into the hole. This should be a tight fit. Place the flush wire flat against the top sheet. Raise the cutters just less than $\frac{3}{8}$ inch (9.5 mm) above the sheet metal, and snip off the wire (figure 2). Do not move the stack. Using a very small ball peen hammer, tap gently around the out side of the extended wire until the top starts to look like a nail head.

fig. 2

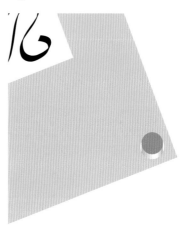

6. Gently turn over the stack, and work the other side in the same manner. Once your first rivet is complete, there will be less shifting and you can then drill the rest of the holes. Work all of the holes in the same manner, and file them so they are smooth and clean. Make at least four rivets in a small piece, and then check for buckling. You may need to add another two to four rivets. Complete as many window rectangles as desired.

7. Smaller items could be lost amid the larger pieces. The solution is to combine several small objects as a single dangle. For example, thread a seed bead onto a 2-inch (5 cm) ball-end head pin, and then stack several small metal disks and washers on top. Finish with a simple loop. Combine items on head pins to create dangles.

8. As necessary, drill holes at the top and bottom of items, attach a piece of 24-gauge base metal wire, and then roll a loop for each hole.

9. The effect of this bracelet is created by using mostly long pieces, combining several smaller found objects to create a longer dangle, and by using many pivot points. Make links by combining several pieces on an eye pin, and then rolling a simple loop at the top. Now you can use a jump ring to attach the top of a smaller, metal rectangle to the bottom of the link. Small springs that you find inside some pens make excellent links: Unwind the very top and bottom of the spring, and wrap each of the ends around jump rings (figure 3).

fig. 3

10. Continue building dangles. You need enough to attach at least one dangle on each side of every link in the bracelet chain. As you work, consider using wrapped loops, rather than simple loops, at the top of some dangles. Simple loops are the easiest, but a triangular wrap will allow a drop bead to move. This will add more visual texture to your finished piece.

11. Use jump rings to attach the clasp to the chain, and then attach the dangles to the chain, again using jump rings.

DROPLETS

Delicate charms and crystals command
attention when grouped along dainty chains.

Instructions

Materials

14 light rose bicone crystals, 4 mm

8 mauve freshwater pearls (potato), 8 mm

2 sterling silver Celtic filigree charms, 6 mm

8 sterling silver flat heart charms, 5 mm

4 sterling silver puff heart charms, 8 mm

2 sterling silver decorative heart charms,
    11 mm

2 sterling silver smooth, flat heart drops,
    10 mm

22 sterling silver head pins, 2 inches
    (5 cm) long

2 sterling silver ear hoops with 3 loops,
    15 mm

24 sterling silver jump rings, 3 mm

7-inch (17.8 cm) length of 2 mm sterling
    silver rolo chain

Tools

Chain-nose pliers, 2 pair

Round-nose pliers

Flush wire cutters

Techniques

Rolling Simple Loops (page 17)

Make two.

1. Cut four pieces of chain 1 inch (2.5 cm) long and two pieces of chain 1⅜ inches (3.5 cm) long.

2. Run a head pin through a bicone, and finish with a simple loop. Add a head pin with a simple loop to the remaining bicones and pearls in the same manner.

3. Open the jump rings. Use one to attach each 1-inch (2.5 cm) length of chain to the left outside loop on the ear hoop. In the following steps, use a jump ring to attach each sterling silver charm or drop to a chain link. Attach each bicone and pearl by opening the loop at the top of the head pin.

4. Attach one of the Celtic filigree charms to the left (outside) loop of the ear hoop.

fig. 1

5. From top to bottom along the chain, attach a bicone, pearl, small flat heart, bicone, and small puff heart in the last link (figure 1).

6. Attach a 1-inch (2.5 cm) length of chain to the right (outside) loop of the ear hoop. Also attach a decorative heart to the right loop of the ear hoop. Add the same bicones, charms, drops, and pearls—in the same order and positions—to this chain.

fig. 2

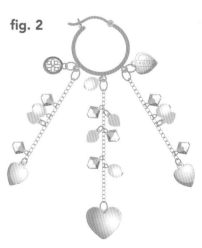

7. Attach the 1⅜-inch (3.5 cm) length of chain to the center loop of the ear hoop. Attach a pearl to this same loop. From top to bottom along this chain, attach a bicone, 3 small flat heart drops, bicone, bicone, pearl, and large heart to the last link (figure 2).

WAVES

Create an undulating tube of herringbone stitch by simply changing bead sizes.

Instructions

1. Thread the needle with an arm's length of beading thread.

2. Attach an 8° stop bead by looping the thread through the bead, leaving a 15-inch (38.1 cm) tail. String 6 Delica beads, leaving 1 to 2 inches (2.5 to 5 cm) of thread between the beads and your stop bead. (The space is needed to make the ladder; it does not need to be maintained once the ladder is completed.) Skip the last bead threaded, and pass the needle through the next bead, going in the same direction traveled when you initially strung the beads (figure 1). Pass the needle through the next bead, this time traveling in the opposite direction (figure 2). Continue in the same manner until the last three beads are worked, so that the beads sit side by side with the holes visible (rather than stacked with the holes facing one other).

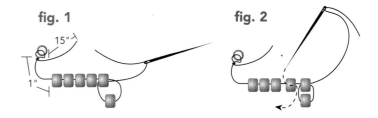

fig. 1   **fig. 2**

3. Swing the start of the ladder around to meet the last bead, taking care not to twist the work. Pull the needle through the first bead in the ladder, and then up through the last bead, to join the ends (figures 3 and 4). Pull the working thread and tail in opposite directions, but do not tie a knot. Leave the tail attached, to form the button loop closure when the bracelet is completed.

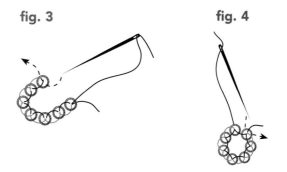

fig. 3   **fig. 4**

Designer: Tina Koyama

Finished size: 6 inches (15.2 cm)

Materials

7 grams of 14° metallic silver or purple seed beads

7 grams of 11° metallic silver or purple seed beads

7 grams of 11° metallic silver or purple Delica beads

7 grams of 8° silver plated or purple seed beads

7 grams of 8° metallic silver hex beads

7 Bali or Thai silver beads, 9.5 to 13 mm

Bali or Thai silver cushion bead, 9.5 to 13 mm

Extra fine, 4-lb. test braided beading thread

Tools

Size 10 beading needle

Scissors

Techniques

Half Hitch Knot (page 20)

Overhand Knot (page 20)

Designer's Tip

To add new thread, adapt the process explained in step 18, except begin by tying on a stop bead, leaving 2 to 3 inches (5 to 7.6 cm) for the tail. Pass the needle up through a few beads about 1 inch (2.5 cm) from the position where you left off. Tie two half hitch knots, pass the needle down through several beads in an adjacent column, and tie two more half hitch knots. Pass the needle up through the beads in the adjacent column, and then pass through beads as needed to position the needle for the next round. Cut off the thread tail close to the work.

4. With the working thread feeding out the top of the last bead worked, string two Delica beads. Pass the needle down through the adjacent bead and up through the next bead (figure 5). Complete two more stitches in the same manner.

fig. 5

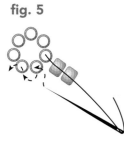

5. To begin round 3, you must step up to the new row by passing the needle through the first bead you added in the last round.

6. Using 11° seed beads, work round 3 by continuing the herringbone pattern established.

7. Work additional rounds of herringbone stitches to create a herringbone tube, changing bead size and type, as noted for your chosen bracelet, in the following table:

	Silver Bracelet	Purple Bracelet
Round 4	8° seed beads	11° seed beads
Round 5	Hex beads	8° seed beads
Round 6	8° seed beads	11° seed beads
Round 7	11° seed beads	11° seed beads
Rounds 8 and 9	Delica beads	Delica beads
Round 10	14° seed beads	14° seed beads
Round 11	Not applicable	14° seed beads

8. Step up to bring the needle into position as if to begin a new round. String one 8° seed bead, Bali or Thai bead, and 8° seed bead. Turn and pass the needle back through the large bead and the first 8° bead. Pull the thread to snug the beads against the herringbone-stitched tube (figure 6).

fig. 6

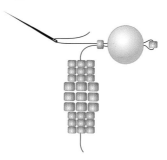

9. Pass the needle down through a few beads in an adjacent column of the tube. Pass the needle back up through the column to which you initially attached the large bead. Continue up—and then back down—through the seed, large, and seed beads in the dangle. Pull the thread snug.

10. Pass the needle down through a few beads in the column where you initially attached the silver bead, and back up the adjacent column until you exit the 14° seed bead at the base of the dangle. This puts the thread in position to begin the next round of the tube in the usual manner (as if the charm was not attached).

11. Continue working herringbone stitches in rounds as noted in the following table:

	Silver Bracelet	**Purple Bracelet**
Round 11	14° seed beads	Not applicable
Round 12	Delica beads	Delica beads
Round 13	Delica beads	Delica beads
Round 14	11° seed beads	11° seed beads
Round 15	8° seed beads	11° seed beads
Round 16	8° hex beads	8° seed beads
Round 17	8° seed beads	11° seed beads
Round 18	11° seed beads	11° seed beads
Round 19	Delica beads	Delica beads
Round 20	Delica beads	Delica beads
Round 21	14° seed beads	14° seed beads
Round 22	Not applicable	14° seed beads

12. Make and attach a second dangle as explained in steps 8 to 11.

13. Continue making herringbone segments and dangles until six dangles are attached.

14. Check the bracelet's fit. The average size wrist will require a seventh dangle followed by one more segment of herringbone rounds. End the final segment after loading Delica beads. With the thread coming out a Delica bead, string an 8° seed bead, the cushion bead, and an 8° seed bead.

15. Turn and pass the needle back through the cushion bead and 8° seed bead. Pass the needle down through several beads in a column. Turn and pass up through all of the beads in the next column. Continue up through the attached 8° seed bead, the rondelle, and the 8° seed beads. Pass the needle back through the cushion bead and seed bead.

16. Pass the needle down through several beads in another column. Tie two half hitch knots. Pass the needle down through a few more beads, and tie two more half hitch knots. Pass the needle through a few more beads, and then cut off the thread close to the work.

17. Turn the piece and thread the tail at the beginning of the work onto the beading needle. If necessary, work the needle through the round 1 beads until the thread exits a Delica bead. String an 8° seed bead. String enough 11° seed beads to fit snugly around the widest point on the cushion bead attached at the opposite end.

18. Pass back through the 8° seed bead. Pass the needle down through a few beads in the column adjacent to the one you exited to start the loop. Pass the needle up through all of the beads in the next column; pass through the 8° and 11° seed beads in the loop.

19. Repeat step 18 around the tube until you have connected all of the Delica beads in the first round to the size 8° and the loop of beads. End the thread with several passes and half hitch knots.

FLIGHT
OF
FANCY

Random bead placement on multiple strands of memory wire lets this piece evolve in unexpected ways.

Designer: Ndidi Kowalczyk

Finished size: 13 inches (33 cm)

Materials

20 to 50 fire polish beads, pearls, or semiprecious stones, 3 to 8 mm

1 brass focal bead, 20 mm

3 to 4 strands fire-polish faceted beads, 6 mm

1 to 2 strands, each at least 16 inches (40.6 cm) long, of garnet-color tumbled stone chips, 3 to 4 mm

6 dove beads (center drilled), 8 mm

4 crystals, 4 mm

1 strand of filed brass cube beads, 3 mm

Vitrail oval crystal, 24 mm

3 to 4 strands pearls (potato), 8 mm

1 antique brass finish bezel cup with loop 20 mm

Locket, 45 mm

6 lockets, 20 to 25 mm

6 small charms, slightly smaller than each locket (except largest locket)

2 biplane charms, 18 mm

2 brass bead caps to fit the brass focal bead

7 head pins, 2 inches (5 cm) long

14 antique brass finish jump rings, 5 mm

2 split rings, 5 mm

Antique brass finish lobster claw clasp

2 antique brass finish 10-loop end bars

2 cone ends, 6 mm

Instructions

1. Use the all-in-one glue to attach and seal decorative and blue paper to the back and interior of the bezel cup and some of the lockets.

2. Place—do not glue—a charm inside the bezel cup and each locket except the largest one. Close the lockets to make sure they will snap shut with the object inside.

3. Lightly coat the interior bezel cup and lockets with the all-in-one glue to attach the charms and embellish them with fire polish beads, pearls, or semiprecious stones. Pour the clear craft lacquer inside each locket.

Stainless steel memory wire necklace with large loops

20-inch (50.8 cm) length of 4 mm base metal cable chain

4-inch (10.2 cm) length of 4 mm base metal cable chain

5-inch (12.7 cm) square of decorative paper

6-inch (15.2 cm) square of blue paper

Water-based, clear-drying all-in-one glue, sealant, and finish

Clear craft lacquer

Tools

Chain-nose pliers, 2 pair

Round-nose pliers

Flush wire cutters

Memory wire shears

Small paintbrush

Small tweezers

Split-ring pliers

Techniques

Using Jump Rings (page 16)

Making Wrapped Loops (page 17)

4. Make a link using the bead caps and the large brass focal bead. Before closing the wrapped loop at the bottom, add a short length of the base metal cable chain. Close the top with a simple loop. Attach the large locket to the bottom of the chain. Create two small dangles to attach along the chain.

5. Make a wrapped loop at the end of a head pin. Cut the head off the head pin. Thread a dove bead and a 4 mm crystal onto the head pin. Make another wrapped loop. Make two more links like this. Use a jump ring to add a locket to the bottom of a dove link. Attach a charm to each of the remaining dove links.

6. Make a wrapped loop dangle on a head pin threaded with a brass cube bead and fire polish bead. Attach this to another link that has only a dove bead.

7. Without cutting off the head on a head pin, make a dangle with a small crystal and dove bead. Using a jump ring, attach 2 links from the base metal chain to the top of the dove bead.

8. Using jump rings, create three dangles by attaching a locket to a ¾-inch (1.9 cm) piece of base metal chain. Make and set aside the following dangles, for use in step 14: Thread a cube and dove bead onto a head pin, and use a simple loop to attach it to the chain on one of the locket dangles. Add a large bead (threaded on a head pin) to another locket dangle. Use a jump ring to add a biplane charm to another locket dangle.

9. Cut a ⅜-inch (9.5 mm) piece of base metal chain. Attach the vitrail oval crystal to one end, using a jump ring.

10. Cut five lengths of memory wire, each with one full rotation plus 3 inches (7.6 cm). Cut three lengths of chain, each 2 inches (5 cm) long, for the spacer bars. Slide an end-link of a spacer bar chain to the center of a length of memory wire.

Designer's Tip

The loops in at least 11 inches (27.9 cm) of the base metal chain must be large enough for the memory wire to feed through. The remaining chain lengths, which are used to join the memory wire loops, can be scrap chain.

11. Add any combination of pearl, cube, stone chip, and fire polish beads to the memory wire, on both sides of the spacer bar chain, ending with a pearl. Continue to string any combination of items until you have covered 1 inch (2.5 cm) of wire on one side of the chain and ¾ inch (1.9 cm) on the other. Slide the top link of the vitrail crystal dangle onto one side and the dove bead dangle on the other.

12. Cover 2 inches (5 cm) on both sides of the chain. Add the next length of spacer bar chain (figure 1). Continue filling the memory wire, for 1 inch (2.5 cm) on both sides.

fig. 1

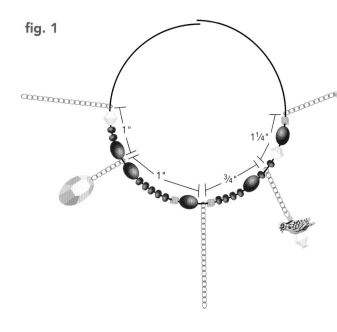

13. Thread another length of the cut memory wire onto the center spacer bar chain, ¼ inch (6 mm) below the link holding the first length of memory wire. String items to cover 2 inches (5 cm) on both sides of the wire (figure 2). Insert the wire through the next length of spacer bar chain. Continue filling the memory wire, randomly adding the dangles you made earlier. Add and cover two more lengths of memory wire in the same manner.

fig. 2

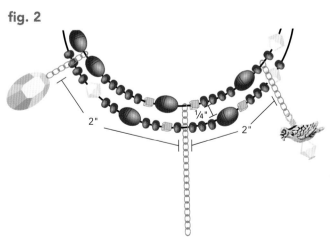

14. Add the last length of memory wire to the central spacer bar chain. String 1 inch (2.5 cm) of pearls and beads to the wire, on each side of the spacer chain. On each side, string one of the dangles that you set aside in step 8. Secure these with several beads and then a pearl. Continue filling the memory wire, randomly adding dangles until just ½ inch (1.3 cm) of the wire remains exposed at the ends.

15. Use the split rings to attach the lobster claw clasp parts to the end bars, adding a biplane charm to one side. Attach the end bars to the necklace, using the round-nose pliers to turn simple loops in the memory wire and connect these to the spacer bar loops. Use the pair of chain-nose pliers to push down on the memory wire loops to close them. Use a 5 mm jump ring to connect a charm or dangle to the last ring of both end bars.

16. Attach the extender chain to one of the split rings. Add a dangle at the bottom of the extender, using a teardrop crystal, head pin, and cone.

HEART TO HEART

Recycling is taken to a new level when old tin gets a new life as bright heart dangles. Just cut shapes from a sheet, rivet, and attach them to your bracelet chain.

Designer: Beth Taylor

Finished size: 7 inches (17.8 cm)

Materials

11 brass or zinc mini eyelets, 3/32 inch (2.3 mm)

22 miniature 0-80 brass and silver-plated, hex or fillister head, bolts, 1/4 inch (6 mm) long

22 size 0-80 brass and silver-plated washers

13 brass jump rings, 8 mm

Brass toggle clasp

6½-inch (16.5 cm) length of 8-mm brass rolo chain

Sheet of tracing paper

Step 1 Templates 1, 2, and 3

2 self-adhesive name badges

8 x 4-inch (20.3 x 10.2) sheet of tin

Clear acrylic spray-on sealer

(Continued on page 94)

Designer's Tip

Avoid tin from soda and beer cans. It is too thin. Tin for your charms should be at least 27 gauge (.36 mm thick).

Instructions

1. Use the tracing paper to copy the heart templates onto the name badges You need five of template 1, four of template 2, and two of template 3. Cut out the shapes with excess paper around each one. Peel off the backing, and affix the shapes to the plain side of the tin. Cut out the tin shapes, keeping the double hearts attached at the tips.

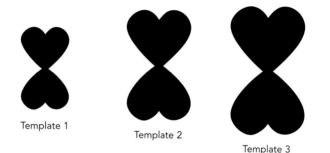

Template 1

Template 2

Template 3

2. Fold each tin heart in half so the two halves are back-to-back and printed tin is on the outside (figure 1). Hammer lightly with the leather mallet to ensure every folded heart is flat. The edges of the folded halves of each heart may not match. Do not adjust them.

fig. 1

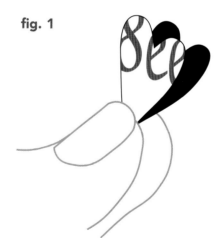

3. With the marker, make a spot for an eyelet at the upper left on one side of each heart. Punch a hole as marked using the two-hole metal punch

Tools

Chain-nose pliers, 2 pair

Wire cutters

Scissors

Fine-tin shears

Leather mallet

Fine-tip permanent marker

Two-hole metal punch for a $^{3}/_{32}$-inch
(2.3 mm) hole

Anvil

Mini eyelet setter

Center punch

4-inch (10.2 cm) scrap of wood

Small clamp

Safety glasses

Drill and #52 drill bit

Flat needle file

Riveting hammer

400-grit sandpaper

Techniques

Using Jump Rings (page 16)

Drilling Holes in Metal (page 19)

4. Insert an eyelet into the hole made in one heart and lay it, facedown, on the anvil. Insert the eyelet setter into the back of the eyelet (figure 2). Holding the eyelet setter with one hand, squarely hit the top of the eyelet setter with the hammer or leather mallet. The eyelet back should curl down, and the eyelet should be tight and secure, through both layers. Set an eyelet in every remaining heart. On each heart, use the center punch and leather mallet to make divots in the upper right and slightly above the point.

fig. 2

5. Place a heart on top of a piece of scrap wood, and hold it with a small clamp (figure 3). Wearing safety glasses, drill holes at each indentation, through both layers. Drill holes in all of the hearts.

fig. 3

6. Thread a washer onto a bolt. Insert the bolt into one of the holes in a heart, through both layers. Snip off the excess bolt, leaving only a tiny amount exposed above the tin (figure 4). File the end of the bolt so the end is flat. Tap around the edges of the bolt with the riveting hammer. The bolt end will flare out and then end up flush against the tin, forming a tight join.

fig. 4

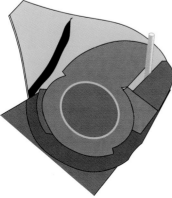

7. Once each heart has been riveted, file the edges until they are smooth and the layers match. File away from you, in one direction only. Finish by lightly sanding.

8. Evenly spray each side with two to three coats of the clear acrylic sealer.

9. Use jump rings to attach each heart to links along the bracelet chain, and to attach the toggle clasp to the ends.

YEE HAW

Antique and embellish new photos and charms for a rustic twist on the traditional themed charm bracelet.

● Instructions

Designer: Deb Trotter

Finished size: 7 inches (17.8 cm)

● Materials

Copper-color seed beads

Multicolor seed beads

2 metal filigree picture frame charms, 30 mm

3 metal photo charms, 40 mm

3 gold or brass western-theme charms, 15 to 25 cm

2 conchos, 1 x 1½ inches (2.5 x 3.8 cm)

2 watch fobs (round), 30 mm

2 brass arrowheads, 1 x 1½ inches (2.5 x 3.8 cm)

13 rusty tin stars, 25 mm

7 western-theme metal or resin buttons (no holes, shanks removed), 15 to 20 mm

2 feathers, 6 cm

2 split rings for every charm and finished dangle

20-inch (50.8 cm) length of 24-gauge copper wire

7-inch-long (17.8 cm) 13 mm link bracelet with toggle clasp

Antiquing solution for metallic surfaces

16-inch (40.6 cm) length each of dark brown, medium brown, and light brown imitation suede yarn; DK or lighter weight

16 vintage photos and pieces of art

8½ x 11-inch (21.6 x 27.9 cm) sheet of high-quality printer paper

Craft chalk

Dark red and brown scrapbooking ink pads

Clear matte fixative spray

8½ x 11-inch (21.6 x 27.9 cm) sheet of scrap paper

(Continued on page 98)

1. Following the manufacturer's instructions, use the antiquing solution to age the metal pieces.

2. Holding the three pieces of imitation suede yarn together, weave the lengths through the links of the chain. Tie the suede in an overhand knot around the last link at each end. Cut the ends to uneven lengths.

3. On your computer equipment, scan the desired photos or artwork, and size the images to fit the conchos, filigree picture frame charms, watch fobs, and both sides of the arrowheads and photo charms. Print them onto the high-quality printer paper. Rub the chalk or scrapbooking ink on the paper images to give them an aged appearance. For fine detail, apply the ink with sponge-tip makeup applicators. Spray the finished images with the fixative.

4. Trace the shape of each concho, filigree picture frame charm, watch fob, arrowhead, and photo charm onto the scrap paper, using a pencil. Cut out these shapes and use them as patterns to cut out the images. Glue the images into the photo charms, picture frames, and watch fobs. Do not glue anything to the conchos and arrowheads yet.

5. Cut pieces of the scrapbook paper to fit the conchos and arrowheads. Tear small bits off the edges to create an aged effect. Color the edges, if desired. Glue a paper piece, right side up, to the back of each colored image. Dab a small amount of clear craft lacquer inside the conchos, and use tweezers to place the artwork on top (figure 1).

fig. 1

6 pieces of decorative scrapbook paper, 1 x 1½ inches (2.5 x 3.8 cm)

Clear drying all-purpose stick glue

Clear craft lacquer

Toothpick

Tools

Long-nose pliers

Micro split-ring pliers

Computer, computer scanner, and photo software (optional, see steps 3 and 4)

Sponge-tip makeup applicators

Pencil

Scissors

Tweezers

Small craft paintbrush

Center punch for a ¼ inch (6 mm) hole and hammer

Techniques

Overhand Knot (page 20)

Note: You may not be able to find some of the exact charms shown in the featured piece. These are found objects that have caught the designer's eye. Use the descriptions—and look at the photos—for inspiration so that you can track down your own special finds.

6. Spread clear craft lacquer over the top of the artwork and onto the surrounding surface of each concho, using the toothpick to smooth the glaze to the edges. Antique the surfaces with the ink.

7. Apply scraps of paper, images, and glaze to both sides of the arrowheads. When both sides are thoroughly dry, use the toothpick and clear craft lacquer to apply the multicolor seed beads along the edges of the images on both sides of the arrowheads (figure 2). Add additional layers of lacquer to create a smooth, protective surface that holds the images in place.

fig. 2

Designer's Tips

Suede-effect yarn that is sold in most craft stores is a better choice than suede or leather lacing, which is too thick. You could use a single strand of leather, but your piece will then miss out on the color and texture that three lengths bring to this piece.

Oversize chain has thick links, and there could be little room between each one. To make it easier to attach charms, connect a jump or split ring to the charm, and then use a second ring to join the piece to the chain link. The charms can shift around a bit more, so you have more space to work between the links.

8. Apply scrapbooking ink to the conchos and arrowheads. Spray the pieces with fixative.

9. Punch holes through the top of the conchos, arrowheads, and rusty tin stars.

10. Use the toothpick to dab glaze on the back of the scrapbook paper and buttons, and then press these onto the filigree picture frames and watch fobs.

11. Cut the copper wire in half. Wrap the end of one piece around the feather, and attach it to the top of a large photo charm. Attach the other feather to the second large photo charm. Slide a small western-theme charm onto one of the wires before wrapping it around the base of a feather.

12. Attach a split ring to the top of every item—including the tin stars—using the long-nose pliers. Use a split ring to attach the rest of the items to links along the bracelet. Add the stars last, as filler. When finished, almost every link will have a charm.

FOREVER YOURS

The most fragile of mementos can become long-lasting treasures
with the clever use of microscope slides and a foiling technique.

Instructions

Designer: Linda Larsen

Finished size: 16 inches (40.6 cm)

Materials

3 crystal beads (flat-back), 4 mm

2 sterling silver rondelle spacers, 4 mm

Aqua faceted crystals (round), 9 mm

5 aqua bicone crystals, 6 mm

5 turquoise nuggets, 5 to 10 mm

5 turquoise cushion beads, 6 mm

Flat, round turquoise nugget, 22 mm

Turquoise pendant nugget, 12 mm

4 brass charms, 25 mm

Brass locket, 18 mm

Found objects: brass zipper pull, piece of
    old tin can, rusted snap, vintage
    jewelry parts, and mother-of-pearl
    wristwatch face and button

Dried hydrangea petal

Postage stamp

Brass locket, 16 mm

16 sterling silver jump rings, 6 mm

8 sterling silver jump rings, 13 mm

Sterling silver jump ring, 13 mm, for the
    button, wristwatch face, and other
    objects to be edged with foil

4 ball-end head pins, 2 inches (5 cm) long

36-inch (90 cm) length of 22-gauge
    sterling silver wire

16-inch (40.6 cm) length of 18 mm sterling
    silver chain necklace with closure

(Continued on page 102)

1. Age all of the brass pieces with the patina, according to the manufacturer's instructions. Glue the flat-back crystals to unexpected places on any of the pieces, such as the front and back of the oval brass locket and the front of the zipper pull. Glue the scrap of fabric to one side of the large locket, and glue a charm on top of the fabric.

2. Set aside the found objects with holes near the top. These holes can be used to add the pieces to chain in a later step. The rest will need to be wired with organic or embellished loops. To make an organic loop, start by cutting the wire for a wrapped loop 4 to 6 inches (10.2 to 15.2 cm) longer than usual. Make the loop and then loosely wrap it, pushing down on the coil with your thumb as you wrap to make it chubby. You can also handle the wire like thread by using a buttonhole stitch to sew around a loop.

3. Don the safety glasses. Score the microscope slide with the glass cutter by running a line at the place you want to cut it to fit the dried and pressed hydrangea petal. Do not continue the score line to the edges. Gently snap the pieces apart by holding the slide on each side of the scored line with your fingers.

Designer's Tips

You can use more than one type of wire to attach your charms. This will add subtle—yet interesting—visual texture to your finished piece. Keep in mind that the wire must be strong enough to withstand the charm's movement when the necklace is worn. You might want to double the loops if you have any doubts about a wire's strength.

Some patina solutions work best if the pieces are left to dry in the sunshine, because the heat helps the chemicals do their job more efficiently.

To give your piece more movement, attach some dangles or charms with large jump rings. These also act as an additional design element when evenly spaced along the chain.

Materials (continued)

18-inch (45.7 cm) length of 1.5 mm
    sterling silver chain

Patina solution for metallic surfaces

Craft glue

1-inch (2.5 cm) square of fabric

2 microscope glass slides

Roll of ¼-inch (6 mm) silver-back copper foil tape

Flux and applicator brush

Lead-free solder

Tools

Chain-nose pliers, 2 pair

Round-nose pliers

Wire cutters

Safety glasses

Glass cutter

Soldering iron

Flux applicator brush

Chasing hammer

Techniques

Using Jump Rings (page 16)

Making Wrapped Loops (page 17)

Note: You may not be able to find some of the exact charms shown in the featured piece. These are found objects that have caught the designer's eye. Use the descriptions—and look at the photos—for inspiration so that you can track down your own special finds.

4. Place the petal between the two pieces of glass. Join the layers by running the foil tape around the edges. Overlap the beginning and end ¼ inch (6 mm). Press the lengthwise edges of the foil tape over the edges of the glass surfaces. Burnish the foil with your thumbnail. Apply the flux. Paint the solder over the tape with the soldering iron. Solder a large jump ring to the top. In the same manner, encase the stamp. Also edge and attach a large jump ring to other found objects, such as the mother-of-pearl button and wristwatch face.

5. Thread the rondelle spacer and large crystal onto a head pin, and complete the dangle with a wrapped loop. Make three of the small bicones into individual dangles using a head pin with a wrapped loop at the top of each one.

6. Secure the small locket to a piece of wire with a wrapped loop. Thread each of the remaining bicones onto separate head pins. Twist the three wire ends together and handle them as a single strand in order to make one wrapped loop (figure 1). Use this same process to create a dangle using three turquoise cushions.

fig. 1

7. Thread a vintage jewelry piece and a charm onto a small jump ring, to make a single charm.

8. Place each large jump ring on a bench block and gently hammer the bottom to slightly flatten them.

9. Select the five largest pieces from the found objects, lockets, and jewelry items. Attach these, evenly spaced, along the center third of the chain, using a large jump ring for each one. Use smaller jump rings to attach all of the remaining lockets and dangles—also evenly spaced—along the center third of the chain.

10. Thread a 2-inch (5 cm) piece of wire through a small nugget, and finish with a wrapped loop. Attach this to one end of the necklace chain, just beyond the last attached charm, using a jump ring. Make a wrapped loop at the opposite end of the nugget, at the same time attaching it to the end of the tiny chain. Wrap and loop the chain through the larger necklace links around the charms, cutting the chain to insert nuggets with wrapped loops as needed to give the necklace a cohesive appearance. (Treat the remaining two turquoise cushions as a single nugget by threading them onto a wire with a rondelle spacer in between.)

11. If desired, secure the fine chain at strategic points along the necklace by threading the chain through an existing jump ring, or attach a jump ring to a necklace link for this purpose. Use another nugget with wrapped loops to secure the opposite end of the fine chain to a link beyond the last charm at the opposite end of the necklace (figure 2).

fig. 2

TRUE LOVE

A necklace with potential gets a facelift with a bit of deconstruction—and then reconstruction—using vintage or new chains, dangles, and charms.

Designer: Erikia Ghumm

Finished size: 16 inches (40.6 cm)

Materials

Word bead, 18 mm

Blue glass bead (round), 11 mm

Pink faux pearl (round) 18 mm

Citrine drop, 13 mm

Pearl (round), 6 mm

Rhinestone spacer, 4 mm

Gray freshwater pearl (round), 3 mm

Crystal drop, 8 mm

Faux pearl charm, 5 mm

Glass heart charm, 9 mm

Glass heart charm, 22 mm

Key charm, 20 mm

Watch face charm, 25 mm

3 sterling silver jump rings, 6 mm

Toggle clasp

6 sterling silver bead caps, 6 mm

4 sterling silver head pins, 2 inches
    (5 cm) long

Sterling silver ball-end head pin, 2 inches
    (5.1 cm) long

5 sterling silver jump rings, 4 mm

7-inch (17.8 cm) length of 16-gauge
    sterling silver wire

26-inch-long (66 cm) gold-color chain
    necklace with heart locket

11-inch (27.9 cm) length of 8 mm faux
    pearl and crystal chain

(Continued on page 106)

Instructions

1. Deconstruct the necklace by cutting off the chain at one side of the locket. On the other side of the necklace, cut off all but 4 inches (10.2 cm) of chain that is closest to the locket.

2. Cut the pearl and crystal chain to three lengths: 1, 4, and 6 inches (2.5, 10.2, and 15.2 cm). Using the larger jump rings, attach part of the clasp to the end of the 4-inch (10.2 cm) length, and attach the remaining part of the clasp to one end of the 6-inch (15.2 cm) length (figure 1).

fig. 1

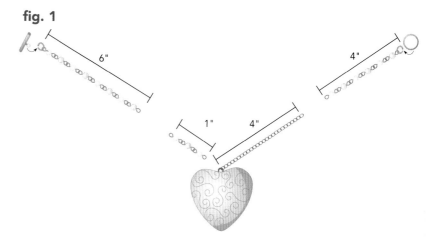

3. Thread the word bead onto the heavy-duty wire. Using the round-nose pliers, make a wrapped loop at both ends of the bead. Do not make this wrap look perfect (see photo below).

Materials (continued)

14-inch (35.6 cm) length of 1 mm curb chain

Piece of plain office paper, slightly larger than the locket

2 photos for the locket

Scrapbooking glue dots

Tools

Chain-nose pliers, 2 pair

Round-nose pliers

Wire cutters

Ruler

Soft-lead pencil

Scissors

Techniques

Using Jump Rings (page 16)

Rolling Simple Loops (page 17)

Making Wrapped Loops (page 17)

4. Thread a bead cap, blue glass bead, and bead cap onto a head pin, and finish with a simple loop. Make two wrapped dangles: On a head pin, thread a bead cap, the large pearl, and a bead cap; on a ball-end head pin thread a bead cap, the citrine, and a bead cap.

5. Slide the small round pearl, spacer, and small gray pearl onto a head pin, and finish it with a simple loop. Use a small jump ring to attach the faux pearl charm to the necklace.

6. Place the paper over the inside of the open locket, and rub over the paper with a pencil to transfer the locket shape. Remove the paper, trim out the shape from the inside, and remove the excess paper to make an opening. Place the opening over the photo, and trace the shape onto the photo. Cut out the shape. Cut a second photo in the same manner. Glue the photos into the locket.

7. Using the two pairs of chain-nose pliers and a jump ring, attach the available end of the 4-inch faux pearl and crystal chain to the loose end of the chain that is still attached to the locket.

8. Open the last link at the available end of the longest piece of pearl and crystal chain. Attach the word bead. At the other end of the word bead, attach the shortest piece of faux pearl and crystal chain. Attach the locket to the other end of this short piece, using a large jump ring.

9. Add the charms and bead dangles to the locket's chain with jump rings.

10. Attach a jump ring to the loop on the citrine dangle, and slide this onto the 14-inch (35.6 cm) length of chain. Add a jump ring to each end of the chain, and use these to attach the ends of the chain to the toggle clasp pieces.

CITY NIGHTS

A pared-down approach emphasizes the clean lines of oversize links on this necklace. The process is so easy, you might want to use the same one to make a matching bracelet.

Designer: Lisa Call

Finished sizes: 16½ inches (41.9 cm)

Materials

7 silver theme beads and charms, 10 to 40 mm

2 faceted quartz beads, 5 mm

Faceted rose quartz bead, 5 mm

White pearl (round), 5 mm

Pink pearl (round), 4 mm

White pearl (coin) 16 mm

Pink pearl (coin) 10 mm

White pearl (flat, square), 10 mm

2 round word beads, 10 mm

Copper charm, 20 mm

Lobster clasp

Sterling silver jump ring for each charm and the clasp, 8 mm

8 sterling silver ball-end head pins, 2 inches (5 cm) long

16-inch (40.6 cm) length of 15 mm circle chain

Tools

Chain-nose pliers, 2 pair

Round-nose pliers

Flush wire cutters

Techniques

Using Jump Rings (page 16)

Rolling Simple Loops (page 17)

Making Wrapped Loops (page 17)

Reaming Beads (page 18)

Instructions

1. Attach the clasp to the last link at one end of the chain with a jump ring. The charm in the last link acts like the finish on a dangle, if you want to adjust the fit by closing the clasp around any link 1 to 2 inches (2.5 to 5 cm) from the end.

2. Thread a jump ring through the largest charm. Attach it to the center link of the circle chain.

3. Thread a bead onto a head pin. Finish the top with a wrapped loop. Use a jump ring to attach the bead's loop to a different link of the circle chain.

4. Set aside the smallest bead or charm for a toggle. Working out from the attached charm and using wrapped head pins and jump rings, add the remaining beads and charms to every second link along the length of the circle chain (figure 1).

fig. 1

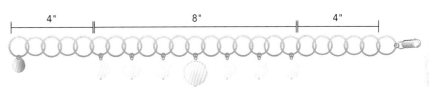

5. Attach the smallest bead or charm to the last link of the circle chain, at the end that is opposite to the clasp.

Designer's Tip

You can use sterling or fine silver head pins in 20 gauge to make these pieces. Unfortunately, this type of head pin is hard to find. With very little effort, you can make your own. Cut a 2-inch-long (5 cm) piece of fine silver wire. Grasp the piece with pliers or locking tweezers, and then place one end of the wire at the tip of the blue flame from a butane torch. The fine silver will melt into a perfect ball without leaving any gray shadows (fire scale) on the surface. Quench the tip in cool water.

WOODLAND

Cascading from a vintage disk, richly colored beads, crystals, and rhinestones dangle on chains of varying finishes.

Instructions

Designer: Bonnie Clewans

Finished size: 4 inches (10.2 cm)

Materials

4 topaz-color prong-set rhinestones with loop, 5 mm

2 topaz-color rhinestone tri-beads (center-drilled), 12 mm

4 bronze-color glass rondelles, 4 mm

2 bronze-color fire polish glass beads, 4 mm

2 bronze fire polish glass beads, 3 mm

4 copper glass nail head beads, 5 mm

2 light gold pearls (potato), 3 mm

2 amber-color crystals (round), 3 mm

Base metal rondelle (flat), 4 mm

2 amber crystals (round), 7 mm

2 jade cubes, 6 mm

2 bronze pearls (potato), 4 mm

2 filigree links, 7 mm

2 black diamond AB glass briolettes, 7 mm

2 metallized leaf charms, 28 mm

2 copper-color filigree disks, 15 mm

8 sterling silver head pins, 2 inches (5 cm) long

14 oval copper jump rings, 5 mm

2 straight-front leg niobium ear wires

6-inch (15.2 cm) length of 28-gauge copper-color wire

6-inch (15.2 cm) length of 28-gauge black wire

(Continued on page 112)

Make two.

1. If you are using new chain, age the metal by brushing it with the black metallic nail polish. Also tone down bright silver wires and the gold backing on the rhinestones with the nail polish.

2. Cut a 3-inch (7.6 cm) piece of copper wire. Make a wrapped loop at one end, at the same time adding a rhinestone in a setting with a loop. Thread a 4 mm glass rondelle and then a 4 mm fire polish glass bead. Finish with a wrapped loop, at the same time attaching the loop to the last link in a 2-inch (5 cm) piece of chain. On a head pin, thread a 3 mm fire polish and a nail head bead. Make a wrapped loop at the top while attaching this dangle midway along the length of chain with the dangle at the bottom. On another head pin, thread a small, light gold potato pearl and an amber crystal, and then wrap the top while securing this dangle 3/8 inch (9.5 mm) from the top of the same chain.

3. Thread the flat rondelle onto a head pin. Insert the head pin through the filigree disk, from back to front, and add the rhinestone tri-bead. Make a wrapped loop on the front, at the same time attaching the top of the chain dangle that you made in step 2 (figure 1). To secure the tri-bead, weave the black wire through the filigree disk and around the rondelle on the back of the disk.

fig. 1

side view

4. Thread a small amber crystal onto a head pin, and attach it to the last link of a 1 1/2-inch (3.8 cm) piece of chain with a wrapped loop.

5. Thread a copper glass nail head bead, glass rondelle, jade cube, and bronze potato pearl onto a head pin. Finish with a wrapped loop, at the same time attaching it to a filigree link bead.

6. Using an oval jump ring, attach a metallized leaf to the last link of a 1-inch (2.5 cm) length of chain.

7. Insert a 3-inch (7.6 cm) length of sterling silver wire through a briolette and finish with a triangular wire wrap, at the same time attaching the drop to the last link of a 1 1/4-inch (3.2 cm) piece of crystal link chain.

Materials (continued)

6-inch (15.2 cm) length of 28-gauge sterling silver wire

6 pieces of silver-color and gold-color 2.5 to 3 mm link chain; 2 lengths each of 1, 1½, and 2 inches (2.5, 3.8, and 5 cm)

2½-inch (6.4 cm) length of 3 mm crystal link chain

Black metallic nail polish

Tools

Chain-nose pliers, 2 pair

Round-nose pliers

Wire cutters

Ruler

Techniques

Using Jump Rings (page 16)

Rolling Simple Loops (page 17)

Making Wrapped Loops (page 17)

Making Triangular Wraps (page 18)

8. Add the chain dangles to the bottom of the disk, attaching each one with an oval jump ring, as shown in the photo below. Also attach the set rhinestone using an oval jump ring.

9. Thread a large amber crystal on the front leg of the ear wire, and attach the embellished disk to the loop.

Designer's Tips

All the chain in this project came from the designer's broken-treasures collection. Be on the lookout for vintage beads at thrift stores and garage sales. You can buy broken jewelry and then take the pieces apart for the components.

When making the second earring, reverse the order of the chains, so that they're mirror images.

NORTHERN LIGHTS

Create dangles to showcase the favorite beads in your stash, and then layer a fine chain swag on top.

Designer: Stacey Neilson

Finished size: 3¼ inches (8.3 cm)

Materials

20 base metal beads, 2.5 mm

Venetian glass bead (round, flat), 20 mm

Dark green bicone crystal, 6 mm

2 yellow bicone crystals, 4 mm

12 lead-free pewter rondelle spacers with fine silver electroplating, 4 mm

Turquoise miracle bead, 8 mm

2 aqua bicone crystals, 6 mm

3 turquoise miracle beads, 4 mm

Venetian glass bead (round), 8 mm

2 aqua bicone crystals, 4 mm

Venetian glass bead (square, flat), 10 mm

2 yellow bicone crystals, 8 mm

Gray miracle bead, 4 mm

Cloisonné tube, 10 mm

Cloisonné drop bead, 17 mm

Crystal teardrop, 12 mm

AB crystal (cushion), 5 mm

Gray round bead, 6 mm

Charm with three holes: one on top, two at the bottom, 15 mm

3 lead-free pewter charms with fine silver electroplating, 6 to 8 mm

6 head pins, 2 inches (5 cm) long

6 base metal bead caps, 4 mm

(Continued on next page)

Instructions

1. Thread a head pin with a base metal bead, cap, the large Venetian bead, cap, base metal bead, the dark green bicone, base metal bead, small yellow bicone, and base metal bead. Roll a simple loop at the top. Join this to the end link of a ½-inch (1.3 cm) piece of link chain. Attach this dangle to the first loop on the pin with a jump ring.

2. Thread a head pin with a base metal bead, rondelle spacer, turquoise miracle bead, rondelle spacer, 6 mm aqua bicone, rondelle spacer, small turquoise miracle bead, and a base metal bead. Roll a simple loop at the top. Use the simple loop to attach the dangle to the pin's second loop.

3. Make another dangle on a head pin, using a base metal bead, rondelle spacer, Venetian glass round, four rondelle spacers, small aqua bicone, rondelle spacer, and base metal bead. Roll a simple loop and then attach this dangle to the fifth loop on the pin.

4. The last head-pin dangle, which is attached to the pin's sixth loop, is stacked with a base metal bead, cap, square Venetian glass bead, cap, base metal bead, cap, large yellow bicone, cap, base metal bead, small turquoise miracle bead, base metal bead, small yellow bicone, and base metal bead.

5. Cut two lengths of beading chain, each 2½ inches (6.4 cm) long. Pinch a crimp to the end of both of the pieces. Drop a gray miracle bead and small aqua bicone down to meet one of the crimps. A quarter of the way up the length, secure another crimp and then a large yellow bicone. The bead will rest on top of the crimp. Pinch another crimp just above the midpoint, drop on the cloisonné tube. Set aside this chain. On the other length of beading chain, drop on a cloisonné drop bead, pinch a crimp below the midpoint, add a medium-size aqua bicone, then another crimp slightly higher, followed by a small turquoise miracle bead. Place the upper end of both lengths of beading chain into a crimp, and pinch it to secure them. Put the crimp joining these two lengths into the open calotte (figure 1). Pinch the calotte closed with the chain-nose pliers. Add the calotte to a jump ring, and secure this to the fourth loop of the pin.

fig. 1

Materials (continued)

7-hole safety pin brooch, 2¼ inches (5.7 cm)

7 sterling silver jump rings, 4 mm

7 sterling silver crimp tubes, 2 mm

Side-opening sterling silver calotte, 4 mm

Sterling silver jump ring (triangle), 5 mm

5¼-inch (13.3 cm) length of 3 mm link chain

6-inch (15.2 cm) length of 0.8 mm beading chain

Tools

Chain-nose pliers, 2 pair

Round-nose pliers

Wire cutters

Crimp tool

Techniques

Using Jump Rings (page 16)

Rolling Simple Loops (page 17)

Using Crimp Beads and Tubes (page 19)

6. Put the triangular jump ring through the crystal teardrop, and pinch it closed with the chain-nose pliers. Open a jump ring and slip the triangle onto it. Temporarily close the jump ring around the last loop of the pin.

7. The last charm is made by adding two miniature earring-style drops into the lower holes of the three-hole charm. Cut four links from the link chain. Open the link at one end to join this piece to the top hole of this charm. Attach the last link to the remaining available loop on the pin. Make two more dangles that you can attach to the bottom loops of the charm. On one head pin, string a base metal bead, rondelle spacer, cushion crystal, rondelle spacer, and base metal bead. On the other head pin, string a base metal bead, rondelle spacer, large gray round bead, rondelle spacer, and base metal bead. Close both head pins with simple loops, and then use these loops to attach the dangles to the bottom of the charm (figure 2).

fig. 2

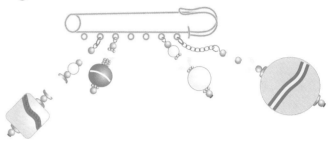

8. Cut a 2½-inch (6.4 cm) piece of chain. Open the triangular jump ring that is attached to loop 7 of the pin. Slip the last link of the chain onto the jump ring.

9. Attach the center of this piece of chain to the fourth loop of the pin, using the jump ring already on that loop. Attach a link near the loose end of the chain to the existing jump ring on the first pin loop, in order to complete the swag. Let the end of the chain dangle below the pin's first loop.

10. Use jump rings to attach a charm to the last link of the dangling end of the chain, and the center of both swags (figure 3).

fig. 3

Bottom layer not shown

TALKING LEAVES

Choose your focal beads and then
let your muse direct the cord weaving
and placement of filler beads.

Instructions

1. Secure one half of the clasp at the 0 on the workboard with a T-pin. Pin the remaining part of the clasp to the workboard at the 7-inch (17.8 cm) mark. (To personalize your bracelet length, pin the remaining clasp at the spot on the workboard that equals your wrist circumference plus ¼ inch (6 mm).

2. Pin the spacer bars to the workboard, evenly spaced between the parts of the clasp. The spacer bars divide the beading area into three equal parts.

3. Set aside the charms and any large beads you plan to use as dangles. Lay out the large beads between the clasp ends and spacers. Place focal items and very special beads toward the center. Lay out the medium-size (6 to 9 mm) beads between the clasp ends, using these beads to accent and complement the larger ones. Place the small beads (4 to 6 mm) next. These bring visual color harmony to the whole composition. Always position a large or medium bead nearest the clasp parts. At both ends of all cords, you need three separate beaded strands to attach to the loops on a clasp. The spacer bars have five holes for threading the cords. This gives you the opportunity to work some portions of beaded strands with doubled cord and larger beads, and then work other portions with the smaller beads on single cords.

4. Surround yourself with small containers of the remaining beads. They will be mixed and randomly added as you string the laid-out beads in the following steps.

5. Cut a length of the nylon cord (either color) to 28 inches (71.1 cm), which is four times the original wrist measurement plus ease. This allows plenty of cord to knot, twine, and finish a line of beads without fear of running short of cord. Cut five more cords to the same length, mixing colors as desired. Finish each end of all of the cords with a drop of craft glue, spreading it thinly and evenly for ½ inch (1.3 cm). When dry, the cord end can act as a needle to pick up smaller seed beads when stringing.

Designer: Louise McClure

Finished size: 7 inches (17.8 cm)

Materials

2 dichroic orange and black glass beads (barrel), 15 mm

Strand green jasper rondelles, 8 to 11 mm

Strand chrysanthemum stone (button), 10 mm

Strand green handmade glass beads, 9 to 10 mm

5 brown glass beads, 9 to 10 mm

Strand horn (golden) rondelles, 6 to 8 mm

3 translucent matte amber glass beads (assorted shapes), 6 mm

Strand peridot smooth briolettes, 5 to 8 mm

Strand green pearls (button), 5.5 mm

Strand amber rounds, 5 mm

Strand peridot faceted rounds, 2 to 3 mm

Strand peridot faceted rondelles, 5 mm

Strand unakite rounds, 4 mm

2 pressed glass leaves, 18 mm

6 sterling silver beads: Rajasthani corrugated moon, 2 bear beads, 3 hill tribes oval leaves, 12 to 15 mm

2 bear fetish semiprecious stone beads, 10 mm

Carved carnelian flower (center-drilled), 14 mm

Carved leaf carnelian (pendant), 25 x 20 mm

Sterling silver charms, 13 to 27.5 mm: leaf, 2 Rajasthani leaves, 2 large arrowheads, 2 acorns, 2 pinecones, feather, small arrowhead

Sterling silver slide-lock 3-strand clasp

2 sterling silver, 5-hole spacer bars, 20 mm

(Continued on page 118)

Materials (continued)

Sterling silver ball-end head pin for each center- and length-drilled bead that will be a dangle, 2 inches (5 cm)

28 sterling silver jump rings, 5.5 mm

6 sterling silver crimp tubes, 2 mm

6 sterling silver crimp covers, 3 mm

Spool of 22-gauge sterling silver wire, dead soft

Spool of light brown 3-ply nylon cord, size #2

Spool of brown, 3-ply nylon cord, size #2

Craft glue with precision applicator

Stick of incense and lighter

Tools

Chain-nose pliers, 2 pair

Flat-nose pliers

Round-nose pliers

Wire cutters

T-pins

Macramé workboard

10 small alligator clips (smooth interior)

Tape measure

Tweezers

Scissors

Crimp tool

Techniques

Rolling Simple Loops (page 17)

Making Wrapped Loops (page 17)

Using Crimp Beads and Tubes (page 19)

Half Hitch Knot (page 20)

6. Select two cords and hold them together as if they were a single cord. Fold the lengths in half to find the center point. Mark this with an alligator clip. Using the layout of the beads on the workboard as a guide, you now begin to string the items, starting in the center of the piece and working out toward one side of the bead arrangement. Still holding the two cords as one, string on a bead, and slide it to the center of the cord. String on several more beads of various sizes, shapes, and colors to form a pleasing composition. Work on a length of 10 to15 mm at a time, splitting the doubled cord to string smaller beads onto a single cord as desired. Use two cords when stringing a large or medium bead. As you work, place an alligator clip on the cord (or cords) next to the last bead, to prevent slippage. Anchor the work with T-pins to keep the cords stable. Stick a T-pin into the workboard where the strands cross, forming an X (figure 1). Size 11º seed beads make great bridges over larger beads on adjacent cords.

fig. 1

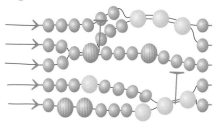

7. When the beading on a cord is long enough to reach a spacer bar, make a half hitch knot beside the last bead threaded. Thread each cord through a hole in the spacer bar, and then slide the bar into position, next to the beads. Knot the cord where it exits from the spacer bar. Knots become a decorative element in your work, but you can hide them inside a bead with a large hole.

8. Continue building your piece until the beaded cord reaches the point where you will add a clasp. Use a large-hole bead next to the clasp. This will help hide the crimp tube and knot that you will use to finish the cord.

9. Slide a crimp tube onto a single cord. Thread this cord through a loop on the clasp, and then thread it back through the crimp tube, thus forming a loop. Push a T-pin through the loop and into board, adjacent to the slide-lock clasp. Gently pull the cord end to tighten the loop. The T-pin will allow a slight bit of ease in the finished loop. Form a half hitch knot next to the crimp tube, and close the tube with the crimp tool. Dab glue on the knot.

10. Clip the cord end ³⁄₁₆ inch (5 mm) from the dried knot. Touch the end of the cord with a lit stick of incense, to melt the end and prevent fraying.

11. Position a crimp cover over the crimped tube, tucking in the molten and cooled end of the cord. Close the crimp cover with the tip of the crimp tool.

12. Finish each beaded cord, attach it to a loop on the clasp, and complete it by crimping as explained in the previous steps (figure 2).

13. Select the center- and lengthwise-drilled beads that you set aside to make dangles. Place each of these beads on a separate ball-end head pin, creating a wrapped loop at the top of the bead. If a bead's hole is large, slip a small bead onto the head pin before—and after—the large bead.

14. Cut a 2-inch (5 cm) piece of wire. With the flat-nose pliers, bend up the last ½ inch (1.3 cm). Thread a top-drilled pendant onto the wire, and then fold up the other side of the wire. Cross the wires above the stone, creating a "hat" for the bead. Take the chain-nose pliers to the base of the longer wire, and bend it back down a bit. Use the round-nose pliers to make a simple loop, and finish the piece by wrapping the wire end around the base three times. Snip off the excess wire and file the end. Prepare the remaining pendants in the same manner.

15. Attach charms randomly to the beaded cords using the jump rings.

fig. 2

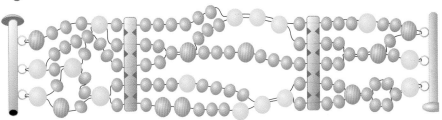

Designer's Tips

The materials list calls for many strands of beads, but you won't need all of the beads from all of the strands. It's a good idea to collect a wide variety, and have them on hand, so that your finished bracelet will look its best.

Fill large-hole beads with 11° seed beads. This will prevent the larger bead from wobbling, which, in turn, will reduce stress and abrasion on the cord.

Use a floss threader, as sold in drug stores, to easily thread multiple cords through large beads, or hollow or filigree beads.

ORIENT EXPRESS

Turn your travel memories into jewelry with this eclectic charm bracelet. Anything will work—from game pieces to old coins. A clever extender quickly transforms the bracelet into a necklace.

Instructions

Designer: Candie Cooper

Finished size: 7½ inches (19 cm)

Materials

1 bead for each game piece, 5 mm

Focal beads and pendants, up to 20 mm

Bead assortment, 4 to 20 mm

9 black glass beads (round), 6 mm

8 cinnabar beads (flat hexagon), 16 mm

2 base metal picture frame charms, 17 mm

Base metal charms, 25 to 44 mm

Base metal head pin for each focal bead,
    2 inches (5 cm) long

Base metal eye pin for each charm,
    2 inches (5 cm) long

2 toggle clasps

2 base metal jump rings, 5 mm

Base metal jump ring for charms and
    dangle, 5 mm

2 silver crimp beads, 2 mm

7-inch (17.8 cm) length of 10 mm base
    metal chain

10-inch (25.4 cm) length of base metal
    16-gauge 49-strand nylon-coated
    beading wire

2 pieces of silk fabric or newspaper,
    or ticket stubs to fit the picture
    frame charms

Chinese replica coin with center hole, 25 mm

6-inch (15.2 cm) length of silk cord

Game pieces and coins, 22 to 26 mm

Craft glue

(Continued on page 122)

1. Slide interesting pieces of fabric, newspaper, or ticket stubs into the picture frames. Connect these to the chain with a jump ring.

2. Thread the cord through the hole in the coin. Wrap one end around the coin and through the hole again. Add a jump ring and tie the cord ends in a knot (figure 1). Use this jump ring to connect the coin to the chain.

fig. 1

3. Continue making pieces, one for each chain link, and arranging them below the chain as they are completed. Do not attach any more until all of the pieces are finished. This will help you establish attractive spacing between the pieces, as well as ensure that pieces look nice next to each other.

4. For coins that need to be drilled, make the hole less than ¹⁄₁₆ inch (1.6 mm) from an edge.

5. Drill ½ inch (1.3 cm) into the top of each game piece. Thread a 5 mm bead onto a 2-inch (5 cm) piece of wire. Make a simple loop at the end. Trim the wire so the loop butts against the game piece when the wire is inserted in the drilled hole. Dip the end of the wire into the glue, and then insert the wire into the hole (figure 2).

fig. 2

6. Thread each focal bead onto a head pin, and finish with a simple loop or wrapped loop. Place a small charm in the loop of an eye pin, and close the loop. String one to three beads onto the pin, and finish with a simple loop at the top. To make a bead dangle, thread an accent bead onto an eye pin, and finish with a simple loop.

7. Connect the toggle clasp to the ends of the chain with 5 mm jump rings. Attach each piece to the bracelet.

Tools

Chain-nose pliers, 2 pair

Flat-nose pliers

Round-nose pliers

Wire cutters

Ruler

Scissors

Safety glasses

Drill and #55 drill bit (optional)

Fine-tip permanent marker

Center punch and hammer

320-grit sandpaper

Crimp tool

Techniques

Rolling Simple Loops (page 17)

Making Wrapped Loops (page 17)

Drilling Holes in Metal (page 19)

Using Crimp Beads and Tubes (page 19)

Note: You may not be able to find some of the exact charms shown in the featured piece. These are found objects that have caught the designer's eye. Use the descriptions—and look at the photos—for inspiration so that you can track down your own special finds.

8. For the extender, alternate stringing one black bead and one cinnabar bead onto the beading wire until you have used the last black bead. String a crimp bead onto the wire, followed by a toggle clasp. Put the same end of the beading wire back through the same crimp bead so that ¼ inch (6 mm) extends out the other side. Crimp to secure the wires, and then trim off the excess wire end to finish one end of the extender.

9. Trim the wire 1½ inches (3.8 cm) past the last bead at the opposite end. String one crimp bead onto the wire, followed by the remaining piece for the toggle clasp. Thread the tail of the wire through the crimp bead. Remove all the slack and crimp.

Bead, Crystal, and Pearl Shapes

This visual guide will help you select appropriate beads for the projects in this book.

Barrel

Bicone

Coin
(or *disk*)

(side view)

Cushion (or *button*)

Cube

Donut

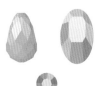

Faceted (3 versions)

Flat

(side view)

Nugget

Oval

Peanut

Potato

Rice

Rondelle (2 versions)

Round (2 versions)

Teardrop

Standard Stone and Bead Sizes

This chart will help you determine the size of an odd bead, found object, or charm that you would like to include in your piece. All the numbers are millimeters.

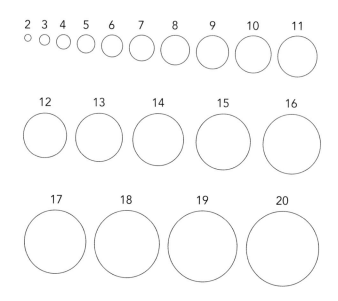

DESIGNERS

Lisa Call has been creating and crafting in an array of mediums her entire life. Aside from raising her girls, wire work and beads are Lisa's main passion. She has spent the last five years focusing on beading and wirework. She is a metalsmith and works with Precious Metal Clay (PMC). Lisa teaches in Seattle, WA, and at the Art & Soul Retreat.

Jean Campbell is a freelance editor and writer who specializes in beading. She is the founding editor of *Beadwork* magazine and has written and edited more than 30 books, most recently including *The Art of Beaded Beads* (Lark Books, 2006), and several from Interweave Press: *Beaded Weddings* (2006), and *The New! Beader's Companion* (2005). Jean has appeared on *Jewelry Making* on the DIY Channel, *The Shay Pendray Show*, and the PBS Channel's *Beads Baubles and Jewels*. She lives in Minneapolis with her family and a whole lot of beads.

Marie Lee Carter tells stories with metal and stone. She has focused on developing skills that allow her to work without the chemicals and fumes of solder, pickle, and buffing compounds. Marie learned her craft by attending classes at the Fashion Institute of Technology and the 92nd Street Y Center, both in New York City, as well as at the Brookfield Craft Center in Brookfield, CT. You can see more of Marie's work at www.mariecarter.com. Marie lives with her husband and son in New York City.

Bonnie Clewans is an international author, designer, and educator. She has appeared on the DIY Channel's Jewelry Making show and local television in Buffalo, NY, and Phoenix, AZ. Bonnie has taught at the Bead&Button Show, International Quilt Festival, Bead Expo, Bead Fest, and the Creative Needlework and Sewing Festival. She serves as a consultant to Swarovski Crystal of North America.

Candie Cooper started making jewelry in high school and has not stopped since. Her passion lies in designing jewelry from unique materials and with vibrant colors. She is the author of *Felted Jewelry* (Lark Books, 2007) and many project designs in various magazines. Her jewelry has been exhibited throughout the United States, England, and Europe. Today, you can find her working and teaching from her studio in Shenzhen, China. To see more of Candie's work, visit her website at www.candiecooper.com.

Gloria Farver often combines beads and fibers in her designs. Her pieces have appeared in *Bead&Button* magazine and *BeadStyle* magazine. Gloria lives in Brookfield, WI, where local galleries and boutiques carry her line. In addition to designing with beads, Gloria enjoys knitting. She can be reached at designsbygwiz@wi.rr.com.

Erikia Ghumm discovered her love for making jewelry as a little girl, when she created her first dried-macaroni necklace. Since then, she has explored many different materials. Nevertheless, still enjoys using found and repurposed items to create distinctive pieces. Erikia is a nationally known scrapbook artist, author, and instructor. Her work has been published in numerous craft magazines and books, as an author, co-author, or contributor. Erikia, who makes her home in Brighton, CO, has a website at www.erikiaghumm.com.

Tamara Honaman is immersed in beads as the media content manager for Fire Mountain Gems and Beads. She has been making jewelry for more than 12 years. She has appeared on the PBS Channel's *Beads Baubles and Jewels* and the DIY Channel's *Jewelry Making*. Tamara is a certified Precious Metal Clay instructor, senior art clay instructor, and is the founding editor of the magazine *Step by Step Beads* and three other publications. Tamara can be contacted at thonaman@msn.com.

Ndidi Kowalczyk is a fashion and surface design artist, with degrees from Drexel University and the Philadelphia College of Textiles and Science. Ndidi was drawn to jewelry design because it is portable and gave her relatively instant gratification. She combines her love of movement, color, and texture to create one-of-a-kind-accessories. Ndidi currently lives in Garner, NC, with her husband and son. She teaches several beading techniques at a bead store in Raleigh, NC, called Ornamentea.

Tina Koyama is a beadwork artist, instructor, and writer living in Seattle, WA. She teaches regularly at Fusion Beads in that city, and travels to teach at national bead shows. One of her pieces is now touring with the Dairy Barn's Bead International 2006 exhibition. You can view more of Tina's beadwork at her website, www.tinakoyama.com.

Linda Larsen started a love affair with color and texture while growing up on her family's farm. She explored a range of arts and crafts until she encountered metalwork, and was smitten. Since then, she has been exploring its limitless possibilities. In 2005, Linda became business partners with Susan Lenart Kazmer.

Susan Lenart Kazmer is an award-winning jewelry designer who works in mixed media, found objects, and metals. Her work has been included in museum exhibits throughout the country, including the Smithsonian in Washington, DC; The Art Institute of New York City, NY; and the Huntington Museum of Art, Huntington, WV. *Lapidary Journal* has said, "Kazmer is a pioneer in the field of patination."

Louise McClure designs her pieces on a battered Gustav Stickley workbench in the western North Carolina mountains. She has put down roots after a lifetime of wandering in Europe, the Far East and the United States. Louise considers jewelry a means of communication, and a vehicle to explore symbolism, history, the mystical qualities of stone, and the psychological influence of color.

Carol McGoogan discovered quilting and the fiber arts more than 10 years ago. Since then, her creative journey has taken her to explore book arts, collage, jewelry making, and metalwork. Her work has appeared in *Cloth Paper Scissors* magazine, and she contributed to *The Adventurous Scrapbooker* (Lark, 2007).

Marlynn McNutt has been the lead jewelry designer for Fire Mountain Gems and Beads for the last four years. During this time, she has created many of the inspirational designs featured on the covers and interior pages of the company's catalogs. An accomplished teacher, she has taught numerous classes for bead shops, small groups, and tours. Marlynn's work has been featured in *Simply Beads* magazine, *Bead Unique* magazine, and several books. She has also appeared on eight segments of the show *Beads Baubles and Jewels*, on the PBS Channel.

Stacey Neilson of Dublin, Ireland, has been beading since she was 12 years old. Her extensive knowledge and design skills were honed by working in many areas of the craft: from owning a retail shop and working at bead shows, to teaching locally and internationally, writing instructions, and designing. Her work has been published in leading American and British beading magazines, *The Beadworkers Guild Introduction* series and several other books.

Beth Taylor is a jewelry designer, metalsmith, and mixed media artist based in Bethlehem, PA. Her work gives new life to found objects such as cultural relics, ephemera, hardware, and vintage tin by making such items into quirky—yet wearable—jewelry. Beth creates jewelry with a sense of meaning, infused with beauty, fun, and funk. Her work can be seen online at www.AQuirkofArt.com.

Terry Taylor is the author of *The Altered Object* (Lark, 2007), *Chain Mail Jewelry* (Lark, 2006), *Artful Paper Dolls* (Lark, 2006), *Altered Art* (Lark, 2004), and a half-dozen other titles published by Lark Books. During the day he is an Acquisitions Editor at Lark Books. In the evening and early morning hours he creates jewelry and mixed media works. He has studied metalworking at John C. Campbell Folk School, Haystack Mountain School of Crafts, and the Appalachian Center for Craft.

Andrea Trbovich, owner of CharmingDarling.com, has loved charm bracelets since she was a child. Corporate life stifled Andrea's creative nature, so she combined her love of charms with her desire to create something artistic and fun, which led to her website business. Andrea lives in Hilliard, OH, with her husband and two charming children. Obsessed with decorating, Andrea moonlights as a home stylist, and occasionally fits in a sewing or painting project.

Deb Trotter uses original drawings and vintage photos of cowgirls, to explore the myth, nostalgia, and humor of the Old West through collage, assemblage, and other forms of mixed media. Deb's award-winning "cowgirl-pop art" has been published in *Cloth Paper Scissors* and *Belle Armoire* magazines, and *Somerset Studio* magazine. Her work has also been featured in the book, *Beyond Paper Dolls* (Stampington and Company, 2006). Her Cowboy's Sweetheart artwork is featured in shops and galleries throughout the United States, Germany, and New Zealand.

Kristal Wick, a Colorado resident, is currently represented by galleries spanning the globe: from Alaska to Europe to the Virgin Islands. With a 16 year career in Corporate America and craving a more creatively fulfilling lifestyle, Kristal decided in 2004 to apply her skills, full time, to the art, jewelry, and fashion world; thus her Sassy Silkies hand painted silk scroll wearable embellishments were born. Kristal also designs and teaches for Swarovski Crystal of North America, and has been featured in over 25 publications.

Index

Attaching charms, 16
Bangle, 43
Basic tools, 15
Beads, 8–11, 16, 18, 37, 85, 112, 119
  Caps, 62
  Drilling, 11, 18, 25, 68
  Shapes, 10
  Sizes, 10
  Stack, 14
Bracelets, 16, 20
Briolette, 18
Brooches, 60
Chains, 8–9, 13, 16, 18, 65, 90, 93, 98, 112
Charms, 8–9, 71
  Attaching, 16
Chevron beads, 62
Clasps, 13–14, 20, 41, 68
Clear craft lacquer, 35
Crimp beads or tubes, 19
Crystals, 8, 10, 19
Dangles, 14, 60, 68, 101
Delica beads, 11
Double knot, 20
Drilling beads, 11, 18, 25, 68
Drilling metal, 19
Earrings, 112
  Backs, 13
Findings, 8, 13, 39, 65
Fire scale, 109
Floss threader, 119
Found objects, 9, 35, 43, 79, 102, 122
Gauge, wire, 12
Half hitch knot, 20, 85
Head pins, 13–14, 16–17, 37, 109
Jump rings, 8, 13-14, 16–17, 25, 35, 60, 98, 101
Knots, 20
Lacquer, 35
Leather, 98
Links, 14, 16
Loops, 16–20, 27, 90, 101
Matte sealer, 29
Memory wire, 12, 90

Metal, 8–10, 65, 80
  Coloring, 29, 80
  Drilling, 19
Necklaces, 20
Nuggets, 62
Overhand knot, 20
Patina solution, 101
Pearls, 8, 68
Pennies, 45
Pliers, 15, 17–18
Reaming beads, 11, 18, 25, 68
Rivets, 80
Seed beads, 11, 119
Settings, 27
Side clasps, 13
Simple loops, 17
Stamp pads, 25
Stop bead, 85
Subway tokens, 55
Suede-effect yarn, 98
Supplies, 15
Techniques, 16–20
Tin, 93
Tools, 15
Torch, 29, 80
Triangular wraps, 18
Wire, 8, 12, 17–18, 62, 101, 109
  Cutters 15
Wrapped loops 17